NUGGETS OF RESURRECTION

Kalu Onwuka

Granada Publishers

Los Angeles, California

Nuggets of Resurrection

Copyright ©2014 by Kalu Onwuka

Published in Los Angeles, California by Granada Publishers. Granada Publishers is wholly owned by Granada Publishing Company, Los Angeles, California.

Granada Publishing titles may be purchased in bulk for educational, fundraising or sales promotional use. For more information please e-mail **sales@granadapublishing.com**

All rights reserved. No part of this publication may be reproduced, stored in a retrieval system or transmitted in any form or by any means-electronic, mechanical, digital, photocopy, recording or any other-except for brief quotations in printed reviews, without the written permission of the copyright owner.

Library of Congress Control Number

Nuggets of Resurrection/ Kalu Onwuka

LCCN-2014911258

ISBN: 978-0-9900203-4-9

ISBN: 00990020347

Printed in the United States

DEDICATION

I will like to dedicate this book, *The Nuggets of Resurrection* which is the first volume of *Ruminations on the Golden Strand* series, to all those who truly share the gifts of light and love everywhere in the world either in formal or informal settings. Yours is not an easy job for truth is very hard to tell and often falls on deaf ears in a world where the sweet and easy has become the norm. The world may or may not acclaim you but Heaven's promise is never to forget or forsake such as you that labor to keep the gate of Light secure against the onslaught of darkness.

ACKNOWLEDGMENTS

As always, I will first like to acknowledge Christ Jesus as the Lord of my life. He is my muse and I write through his light. Also, I will like to acknowledge that it is not possible to see through an undertaking such as *Ruminations of the Golden Strand* series without the loyal support of family, friends and well-wishers. You have all been there from the beginning through to the publication process. I will like to acknowledge all your assistance for you continue to give me cause to hope for the best in mankind. It is such goodness that you show that will help to transform the world from what it is today to the better that it can become in the future.

CONTENTS

Dedication   iii

Acknowledgments   iv

Introduction   vii

Chapter 1   Driving Wisely in Life   1

Chapter 2   In Light and Wonder   13

Chapter 3   For the Pure of Heart   27

Chapter 4   Still Small Nuggets   37

Chapter 5   From Perch of Mercy   47

Chapter 6   Urge to Re-Create   59

Chapter 7   The Living Church   69

Chapter 8   Within the Divine   81

Chapter 9   Faith-Rest into Restoration   89

Chapter 10   Mercy Brings New Life   103

Chapter 11   Death to Afford Peace   115

CONTENTS

Chapter 12	The Golden-Hearted Shine	125
Chapter 13	Where Heaven meets Earth	133
Chapter 14	Birth-Pains of the New	145
Chapter 15	A Reclamation Project	155
Chapter 16	A Passport is Required	165
Chapter 17	A Network of Hope	175
Chapter 18	In Steps of Mercy	183
Chapter 19	The Sharer Abounds	191
Chapter 20	The Meat is the Life	203
Chapter 21	Offspring of Wisdom	213
Chapter 22	Rejected but Worthy	223
Chapter 23	Cloak of the Mighty	233

INTRODUCTION

This book titled *Nuggets of Resurrection* is the first volume in the *Ruminations on the Golden Strand* series. While this expansive discourse explores the many gifts available to the faithful believer through Christ Jesus, it also points out the challenges to be faced along the way and presents the reader with ways to overcome inevitable obstacles.

In life, it is said that victory favors the well-prepared. In as much as the journey of faith avails much blessing, the truth is that it is filled with trials and challenges. The upward way is much like a distillation process that serves to rid mankind of earthiness so that the spirit within can rise to the utmost or heavenly side of being. The latter is the place of regeneration reserved for those who faint not or weary not along the way to become fully matured in spirit and be deemed worthy of the passport to eternity with God. It is also the spiritual state where the needful things that may have been lost along the way are restored within a better light of understanding.

The man that is not fully matured in spirit may walk in some measure but he will not walk in the fullness of light to receive all the gifts available through Christ Jesus. Only he that walks in fullness of light can be tuned in spirit with the Divine to be guided into regeneration. Regeneration is a time of a new dawn in a believer's life when everything that he touches will seem to turn into gold. The believer that is in regeneration will have the ability to see and think from a heavenly perspective. As a result, such will be inspired to do many things exceptionally well.

Regeneration is a spiritual state that can be known only when the heart has become pure. The heart can never become purified except through the fire of trials so that man can learn to fully trust and become subservient to the Divine will. The regenerative state reveals itself to the pure of heart that lives by Truth but conceals itself from the heart wherein darkness still lurks. The purer that man's heart becomes is the clearer that his spiritual vision becomes so that he will not only begin to understand self and surroundings better but the greater realm beyond the flesh as well. All who faithfully walk in true light are often battered and bruised by the assault of a world that often rejects them as contrarians. But through those assaults come a renewal in mind as well as growth in spirit that leads into a fuller and deeper understanding of God. It is this roasting in the fire of the spirit that leaves an indelible mark on the faithful soul to brand him as belonging with God and leads into regeneration.

To be in regeneration is to dwell on a spiritual housetop or the summit of faith. It is a place reserved for those who have been able to let go of the world and so are lifted in spirit into that higher realm that eludes many. It is from the vantage point of the housetop that the eye of the spirit can be truly focused on God. From there, the faithful is able to perceive that which is beyond the horizon to become a discerner of the future, harbinger of the new and an agent to be used to transform humanity for better. All things in creation originated from God's all-knowing mind and came into being through his divine impulse. It is this ability to create that the heavenly Father avails through regeneration to the fully matured in spirit as he dwells on the spiritual housetop.

As a result, all who have been availed such minds are able to re-create their little plots on earth into a garden after the order of things in Heaven. It is the same spirit that created the grand universe that is at work in them through regeneration to re-create their earthly allotments with the divine aesthetic. The mind, pattern and motif are similar but differ only in scale. All who are able to recreate the heavenly on earth in this manner are in effect extensions of the heavenly Father. Such are the faithful ones within whose hearts the Divine dwells and through whom heavenly wonders come to be displayed on earth.

The truly faithful in Christ are often rejected by not only unbelievers but by many professed believers as well. Many in the world are spiritually blind and therefore unable to understand the life of the believer that is fully matured in Christ. Sadly such is often viewed as having lost his mind and considered strange for he walks on the path less travelled and not on the well beaten tracks that most love.

Introduction

Nevertheless the earthly handiworks of the man in whom Christ has come to full spiritual maturity will reflect the changes that has undergone within him. As a man's state is within him, so will his estate without be. For this reason, as the spirit within him is progressively transformed, man's handiworks on earth also changes from the ordinary to the exemplary that shines with distinction as an indication that the Divine is at work therein.

Remarkably, the spiritually matured in Christ comes into regeneration to dwell in assurance and certain peace under divine mercy that is not determined by life's circumstances. It is peace that is hard to explain to the casual observer. It comes from the death of the old self that sometimes strove against God in the past. With the death of the old self through spiritual maturation, a new comes to life that no longer strives against but yields to God's divine will. Such that is reborn as new no longer strives against but is with God in communion of spirit and called to live with compassionate love for all.

The fully matured in spirit is given to ascend to the exalted realm where heaven and earth meet in love. It is the heavenly side of earthly living that mankind realizes by communion with the Divine. The compassionate soul is exalted to become a courier of God's precious seeds and given to walk under divine sunshine. The precious seeds of God are the seed-thoughts for works that are ordained in Heaven to be done on earth below. Such precious seeds are usually entrusted to a chosen vessel and serve to further the kingdom of God on earth. The chosen vessels are those hearts which have been lit with the flame of love for humanity through Christ. Such are Heaven's trustees guided to plant in the right seasons and in fruitful grounds.

It is through the couriers that divine power manifests mightily to do wondrous works among mankind. It is power that only the pure of heart and noble of soul ever get to know and experience. The life of the pure of heart and noble of soul is anchored on Truth. Such never wanders far from the laws and commands of God. As a result, he will reach a point in time when he becomes the words of Truth even as the words become him. It is at this point when the faithful seeker in the footsteps of Christ becomes the embodiment of Truth that he is connected to the universal mind of God to shine as light. All such who embody Truth are not only reborn to shine as light but are given new names as members of the divine household.

The members of the divine household are in the world but no longer of it for they dwell on the heavenly side of earthly existence. All who dwell there are able to receive due knowledge and help needed to overcome in life. Such are duly informed about important issues of the present as well as the future that require attention through the gift of the Holy Ghost. Every one that receives information in this light can be likened as having insider information about the important for it seems as though a little bird whispers

Introduction

into his mind. Such is one fed with the data that he needs in order to be well-prepared for victory and to live in harmony with all around him. The entity that avails this information is the Holy Ghost. 'He' is highly necessary for victorious living but availed through mercy to the pure of heart and noble of soul tuned in spirit to hear.

Nothing must choke the channel of mercy for it must remain a freeway of love where light and life can fully abound. The channel of mercy is the highway of the free in spirit who has overcome the world to ride in the exalted place where only few can venture. Mercy is the best well reserved and asks of the believer to make that last sacrifice so that he can be received into the realm where mankind reconnects with the Father to partake in heavenly conversations.

Worries, cares, grievances, resentments, grumblings, anger, envy and such emotional malware slowly but surely drag down the spirit into a stall. The stalled spirit cannot ride on the high places but the low places of the earthly. Such soon vacates the place of honor appointed for him. The light of Christ abounds by being thankful for that received, sharing, and bearing testimony about God's goodness to mankind. He that will not bear testimony and give thanks for the gifts received will not be fruitful in the way. Such does not acknowledge grace and will not come under divine mercy. Such has not used well that which he has been given and therefore will not receive more.

Introduction

Lastly, mankind should always bear in mind that the world's system is born of the tree of good and evil. It is a way of living that sadly measures progress and defines itself by the things that show up to great applause as being good in the beginning but which eventually turn out to be less so with the passage of time. Consequently most of man's undertakings are crowned with decay and death reigns all around him. In that regard it all seems to be a waste of time and efforts until man the creature learns to yield control to be guided in his endeavors by God his Creator. It is indeed best for mankind to yield to the all-knowing potter that fashioned him who knows best his place on earth and best role to play. It is the only way for mankind to find fulfillment.

This book is not a substitute for the Holy Bible but only serves to amplify the eternal truths contained therein. As the reader ruminates through this volume, I hope that the truth laid bare within the pages will help enlighten minds and reshape hearts into vessels of honor that serve the Divine in truth and love so that humanity can become collectively better.

Kalu Onwuka

The sun always gives to such

That opens in warm embrace

Offers up the life giving rays

To anyone who fears not light

Chapter 1

THE WISE DRIVER

The truth about the life of faith is that it takes full spiritual maturity to walk under the greater or full divine light. The man that is not fully matured in spirit may walk in some measure but not in the fullness of divine light. Only the believer that walks in full light can be tuned in spirit to know the Divine will always. Consequently only the matured in spirit can truly tarry for directives from the heavenly Father before proceeding on a course of action. Such is one who has learned by experience that much goodness attends when mankind faithfully yields to be led in spirit by the Divine. The believer that has learned to yield in this wise will come to dwell under mercy where divine blessing attends earthly endeavors.

The believer that dwells under mercy has come into a spiritual communion with God. It is when the believer has matured in spirit to always be in communion with him that God readily hands over the reins of divinity to mankind. It is the foretaste of heavenly glory where God in effect anoints mankind to be the vehicle to help his divine designs come about on earth. It also means that the believer has become adopted as a son of Heaven to go about for God on earth as his earthly representative. To be handed the reins is like the father giving the keys of the high powered expensive family vehicle to that son who has proven to be a trusted driver on the road of life.

The believer becomes a trusted driver when he has learned the code of the road of life by driving some inexpensive low powered vehicle. He has learned to drive safely by following the driving manual of biblical laws and commands. In that way, he is one who has proven worthy of the little and so can be entrusted with much. Such becomes privy to knowledge deemed mystifying by others. In effect, he has progressed from the lesser light availed to all comers to the greater light availed only to the worthy. He has become one that can be accounted as a minister of the gospel of Christ and also a custodian of the mysteries.

As aforementioned, the faithful one who has been proven and deemed to be a worthy driver on life's harrowing road can be trusted to drive the family's high powered prized performance vehicle. The vehicle is the divine wind and it is available as needed to the faithful and worthy driver. The worthy that asks can have the vehicle anytime when needed as long as it is for family business of helping humanity. It is important to always ask for permission from the heavenly Father as well as state the reason for needing the vehicle. It is divine to ask for he that asks not violates the way. To ask is to honor the Father who gives good gifts to mankind as due. The true believer knows that there is to be no violation in light and never fails to ask. He knows to ask through petitions and prayers in all things.

For man to have access to the divine vehicle is a grand investiture as it makes possible the accomplishment of things that would otherwise be impossible for mankind to do on his own. For instance, he that has the key to the vehicle can travel to the distant abode of the stars in spirit where the golden star dusts rain and the lamp of genius can be touched. He can travel to the place of the rain clouds in order to restrain the floods that spiritually ravage the land. He can also travel there to call back the rains to refresh the parched land and make the desert bloom again. To travel in spirit in this wise is to have the desires of the heart readily granted by prayer and petition.

Such an anointed traveler in spirit has been entrusted with a special divine gift to restore life to the withered and dying. Such is a regenerator of life who collects and brings down the dew of mercy from heavenly to earthly places. For all intents and purposes, he can be likened to an alternator who draws from the eternal dynamo of Heaven to recharge hope into an exhausted earth. But the divine vehicle is more than that for it also serves another purpose. It is a rescue vehicle that the son who has been entrusted with the key can use to rescue those who are lost on life's way and seek to rediscover purpose. When used for rescue in this wise the vehicle becomes a family car. But it is not for joy riding but for running life's important errands. The most important errand of all is to pick up those that are lost and stranded in the world in order to bring them back on the road that leads home to the heavenly abode.

Man becomes lost in the world when he no longer counts God as part of life's equation in his lust after worldliness and thereby loses his connection with the Divine. Many are lost from trying to take short cuts in life, others from living by sight and following after crowds. Yet there are those who have been misled and lost their way due to lack of knowledge and spiritual blindness. Many are the reasons but the outcome is the same sad one of hope lost. All who are lost on life's treacherous way can be rescued if they are willing to receive help for all are welcome to come aboard the divine vehicle. The token required to get on board is belief and faith in the redeeming power of Truth to save mankind by grace through Christ.

When the divine vehicle is used for the rescue of the lost, the driver can then be likened to a sun and all who have joined him on the vehicle as planets. In this way, each son or driver becomes a 'sun of righteousness' around which revolves some planets drawing from the life giving energy that he receives from the heavenly Father. In this spiritual family, each sun of righteousness or son of God is likened to a bridegroom and the planets that revolve around him are like maidens expected to bear children. Every maiden that bears a child in the way of light shall be saved. To bear a child requires that the believer tarry in faith to be spiritually matured for only such can conceive to bear the fruit of righteousness. To bear fruit is to share Truth and live by good example in Christ so that others can come into the light and knowledge of the Divine.

Life is the essence of the everlasting. As such every planet or maiden that harbors and nurtures life is given to be everlasting. Such will always be regenerated from one age into a new one in the fullness of time when the present is no longer sustainable. Regeneration is the emergence of new and better life from the carcass of the old. The divine soul is eternal and regeneration is for those who have come into full spiritual maturity in light as well as for the believers 'married' to them in spirit who have borne good fruit in the way. To be married in this sense is to join up with one in spirit. It is not a physical but an unbreakable spiritual bond with the aim of producing offspring that is purified of soul and lofty in spirit. Those who have come into full maturity in Christ are in spiritual communion and can interact with the heavenly Father.

There is no longer the fear of death when new life has been realized from the old. On the other hand, the better begins to emerge from the former in all life's endeavors. All who have come to full maturity in Christ become reborn as sons of God in divine light and the maidens that are 'married' to them through the embrace of Truth are duly awakened to grow in spirit within. Such come to be filled with the sweet wine of new life through the sons. The words of the sons wash the souls, purify the hearts and fill the 'maidens' who embrace them with the living water of the spirit of life through grace. It is the living water poured into the 'maidens' that turns in due time into the sweet wine of a new life availed under mercy.

Those who are reborn in light are revealed and best recognized in the season of humanity's nighttime. This is when light has dimmed and there is pervasive darkness that leads many to lose their way in the world. There is no question that darkness has enveloped the collective soul of humanity today. The human spirit despairs and there is palpable fear in the hearts of many. But pervasive human weaknesses and failures always set the stage for the mighty power of God to be displayed. It is when the humdrum is run out that the better and sweeter is availed.

Christ Jesus is the first born son and the 'Savior of saviors'. All who are reborn in light are the sons of God duly prepared as the 'saviors' of mankind to take men forward from darkness into light. Such are the sons of men divinely invested with the power to serve Heaven and earth as sons of God below. There are many sons positioned all over the world to serve as stars to guide the seeker in today's world that is a sea of darkness. All the sons are in spiritual communion with God which enables them to act as one through Christ by the love of truth and light.

There are many such 'saviors' positioned all over the world. They act with a common purpose to help bring about God's will on earth. Collectively all the sons aggregate as one savior for the sons reign together as one to serve God's divine purposes on earth. They are all yoked together with Christ Jesus and plow garden earth in accordance with the heavenly Father's wishes. The Divine mind can create the special out of the ordinary, set order out of the chaotic and bring new life out of the dead. The heavenly Father has the power to make much happen on earth. By extension, the sons worthy of him can do much in God's name for he wills and acts through them.

The reborn in divine light are duly led in spirit into a place where the means to realize all their needs are provided. This place where Providence is at hand affords mankind a platform to realize his visions through Christ. It is the place for those with great vision and strong faith. Each son is called by God to stand on that platform and show forth that for which he has been prepared. He is called to repair the breaches that the prince of darkness has made by removing the obstructions so that the sunshine of divine love can reach farther and further. He is called to rebuild the bridges, heal the broken hearted and lift up the down trodden for he has become a dwelling place of the heavenly Father on earth.

The reborn in Christ is a son of mercy who is called to pray for forgiveness for the ignorant and be the vehicle used to extend the Divine way on earth. There are many that transgress God's laws due to either ignorance or willful disobedience. The Father asks his sons to beg for mercy and forgiveness not only for themselves but most importantly for the many others who know not what they do. Each son is never to withhold mercy from those who ask for he is an agent for bearing children from the world of darkness into light. Therefore they are called to make sure that all who sincerely seek redemption get a good chance to find it. All that come in true penitence are to be forgiven and well-received for that is a mark of Divinity.

Chapter Notes

- ✓ God lends the key of the divine vehicle to the believer who drives prudently on life's road.
- ✓ The driver receives the key by request through prayer and must use it to make humanity better.
- ✓ The divine vehicle is the purified soul of the believer riding on the wind of the spirit of God.
- ✓ The spiritual union forged in love produces an offspring that is purified of soul and lofty in spirit.
- ✓ God's redeeming power is best displayed in seasons of human weaknesses and failures.
- ✓ The matured in spirit have a platform to realize visions and the means to transform the world.
- ✓ Divine blessing is bestowed when the heart of the believer is in tune and at rest with God.
- ✓ The believer in tune with God is in tune with the universal language of life.
- ✓ The believer that is in harmony with creation has been duly appointed a room in God's mansion.
- ✓ The believer must have peace within the soul in order to be certain in faith to take orderly steps.

Regeneration begins at point of escape

From the misguided and misgiven past

Tis much like the welcome face of dawn

A break that follows an unending night

Chapter 2

IN LIGHT AND WONDER

Every believer that matures in spirit through a faithful relationship with God and whose mind dwells on the uplifting things will come into a season of regeneration. The season of regeneration is the time of a new beginning in a believer's life when all which he touches will seem to turn into proverbial gold. This is when he will begin to do many things exceptionally well. This comes about from the ability to see and think from a divine perspective as well as having the aid of an unseen heavenly host. It is a season when the faithful believer is inspired in many ways to produce such works that shine before men to God's glory. It is a time when the greater and fuller light dawns in the life of those that truly serve God's will on earth.

Regeneration begins at the point of total escape from the misguided and misgiven past. It is like the welcome break of dawn that follows a nightmarish night. The light of this new dawn is ideal for the believer to realize and nurture many spiritual gifts. Regeneration is ideal for the little seed with God in it. No other manner of seed will thrive under its judging and proving light. It is light that offers evidence that the spring of a grand awakening has finally arrived in the believer's life. Only those who have believed and kept faith with Truth in love awake to this light.

Such who have waited in hopeful belief become witnesses to all that God has promised mankind in love. They waited in hope for the time of fulfillment when the womb of the new dawn will open so that they can ascend to the higher and purer. They waited for the time of full manifestation when the power of God will be fully displayed to aid their endeavors. They waited for rebirth from the earthly to the heavenly. They waited for the new beginning destined for those who have found peace in God.

The faithful believer that comes into regeneration is a son of God equipped to do much good but the power to switch on the light for humanity's new age lies in a critical number of them. One son will chase a thousand but an adequate number of them will irreversibly change the world. God is always searching, choosing and adding sons to his divine household. The sons are chosen from all over the earth from different colors, countries, tribes and tongue. The tree of life produces a different manner of fruit each month and so a son is chosen even as the moon shows its full face every month. A son is chosen and added to the count until a critical number is reached that only the heavenly Father himself knows.

It is Heaven's choice alone and mankind has no say in the matter concerning the choice of the sons except to yield his heart when God calls. The sons are paired in twos and work together as binary star systems. There is always a son that is in the lead and another that brings up the rear. The son that is in the lead reaches out and receives from the future. The son that brings up the rear keeps the past at bay so that what has been received from the future can be shielded from that which will corrupt it from the past. For instance the son that hears with certainty is paired with one who is fearless. Certainty makes for great vision and courage strong faith. The son that hears declares Truth with unequivocal certainty. He is the one that gives voice to that heard by faith which comes from beyond the heavenly throne to shine light on earth. On the other hand, the son that is fearless always finds a way to move the mountain that aims to shield the light and keep mankind in shadows or total darkness. Both sons make the pair that never gives up and perseveres to the end.

Both sons work together to conjure up the diamond spearhead that pierces through the flinty rock. It is a spearhead because it pierces the resistive to take man beyond the boundary of the hitherto known into that yet to be known. It is a diamond because it cuts across the whole world and through humanity to evoke the ever-increasing kingdom of Christ with nothing to stop it. Such is the spiritual dance of the matured or elder in faith with the yet to mature or younger. It is evoked and sustained by the heavenly dynamo that pulses endlessly through time. In the appointed season, the young becomes the elder and the elder is reborn into a young one. It is the Spirit of God that wills and acts through both to determine the due time to switch places. It is the ring of creation from which new life is spawn. It is death swallowed up by life or rather life mocking death.

The spiritual bond between the elder or matured and the younger or maturing is never broken once formed. This is the perennial dance of time in which the wonder of eternity is displayed. The emblem of this rebirth is the hourglass where one half empties into the other until it is turned over at fulfillment of time by divine mandate to begin a new spiritual sunrise. The lead changes within the spiritual bond at the moment of turning over when the younger becomes the elder and the latter is reborn as the young. The old has yielded to the new in this order of enlightenment through Christ.

There is momentary silence in Heaven when the hourglass is turned over but it is soon followed with great joy for it signals regeneration and dawn of the new age for the reborn in light. It is all by heaven's mandate and destiny's call. The new age is filled with peaceful hope and bubbles with magnanimous optimism. It is the grand awakening of humanity into its purified better. It is the ugly waking up to find itself beautifully transformed in the divine mirror. It is the saga of the ugly duckling turned into a beautiful swan that glides in majestic control through life. It unfolds from glory to more glory as time elapses. In this glorious dawn, everything gets better with the passage of time contrary to what the world's way offers mankind. It is the irrepressible combination of the elder and the younger in the bond of light that keeps the way open to make possible the spread of the kingdom of God.

Each son bears up the other so that the strength of one shores up the weakness of the other. It is two imperfect things mixed together with a pinch of divine salt to manifest that which is perfect. It is this search for the perfect that urges on the spread of light. It is this wisdom of the highest order that turns human weaknesses into marvelous strength much like carbon is transformed into diamond. The bond between the elder and the younger in spirit is the embodiment of that perfection much sought after but which still continues to elude humanity. It is that which always seems close but yet remains fleetingly out of reach for the most part. It is that which can only be realized through Christ.

Such unions of the elder and younger in the way of Christ

have been paired up and positioned by God all over the world. It is a thousand points of light coalescing into one great light. It is the dance of light to shame darkness into oblivion. It is the light of the flames that glows from the hearts of the sons joined in such unions that will blend together into the great dawn of humanity to bathe the world with the essence of Christ.

The essence of Christ is truth, light, love and the everlasting. The great dawn will be the realization of the reign of the kingdom of God on earth through the light of Christ. It is the moment of the twinkling of an eye when all shall be changed and death will be swallowed up by life. Such is the essence of regeneration and it is that which the whole creation has been hungering for. It is the better light by which mankind can cast his net in the world and have a good reward for his efforts without disappointments. He will be protected from disappointments because he casts in full light with an informed purpose and can therefore bring in the desired harvest every time to divine glory.

The faithful that has come into regeneration is a son of Heaven who has been well-prepared and equipped for the mission of Christ. He has become connected with the Divine mind to join the conversation in heavenly places which makes all things affordable and within reach. He has been given access through the power of prayer as the means to ask and receive without fail from Heaven. There is much power availed to the reborn in light but it can only be unlocked through petitions and requests made to God through prayers. It is power made available through Christ, with the Holy Spirit and for God's glory. It is power availed to the man who truly loves and gives due honor to God in all his undertakings. He that has been reborn in this light is a son who need not labor any more by his own devices for he can have much more accomplished in all areas of life through divine help. He has been given access and can summon a spiritual host to aid him unlike the faithless man who is left to labor alone in his own understanding.

In order to make the most effective use of the power of prayer, the petitioner must be mindful to desire those things that will please God. He has to earnestly invite the Holy Spirit to take the lead in all his endeavors and never fail to give God due thanks. It is not that God does not know what the son needs or craves praise. It is just that asking for it brings a measure of accountability into the relationship between creature and Creator. God grants the prayers of the faithful believer but the latter must live for the cause of love and goodness with charity as life's true calling. His motive must never be for personal gain but to serve humanity in love for by so doing will he be worthy before God to be richly blessed in many areas of life.

There are many who profess to follow after the footsteps of Christ Jesus who partake unworthily of grace availed thereby. For such the walk after Christ is for personal gain and not for the cause of love and goodness. There is an appointed time when grace runs its course. It marks the transition from spiritual childhood to manhood. When that time comes about, the faithful is ushered into the place of mercy before God. Mercy endures forever and it is for the few given to come into eternal life. The unworthy partaker of grace will never come into mercy for he will be stuck in spiritual immaturity for setting the divine feast to naught. He is one who has chosen filthy lucre and opted to serve the mammon of unrighteousness above God. The allure and abuse of grace has led many professed believers to unwittingly invite darkness into their lives.

Many who claim to walk in the way of light after Christ have become corrupted in spirit on account of addiction to grace. Grace is supposed to be a means to an end. Grace is transitional and not the end of spiritual quest. It is full spiritual maturity through grace on to mercy that is the desired end. In selfishly gouging themselves with grace, misguided believers have risked missing out on mercy which is enduring and salvation which is eternal. They have chosen to become bloated in the flesh but under nourished in spirit. Such have failed to understand that the flesh has to be pared for the spirit to flourish.

There is however an appointed season when grace is withheld from the unworthy. The end of the window of grace represents the beginning of pre-judgment within the body of fellowship that professes to walk in light after Christ. As the window of grace closes, the door of mercy is opened so that only those able to stand firmly in faith can walk in. The infirm spirit has no spiritual legs and cannot step into the realm of mercy for he cannot walk. The close of the window of grace is a season of spiritual self-examination divinely purposed to reset the heart so that the mind of the true seeker can refocus on God.

The believer that is enamored with and stuck in grace will be in an arrested spiritual development. There are many ways in which arrested spiritual growth manifests itself. The believer that is in arrested spiritual development cannot be weaned away from the milk of the word even though the season for him to be able to eat the meat of the word has come about. He is not able to study and understand the word of God by himself but still relies on another to teach him when he should be the one to teach others. He is not able to grow into a greater understanding of God but only regurgitates the old standards for he is not able to join the conversations in heavenly places. He cannot bear true testimony about the power of God for he has little experience of divine power that he can truthfully attest to.

The spirit of God is progressive and always brings new things out of the old. True faithfulness asks of the worthy believer to pour out himself selflessly into others that lack so that they may come to know and see in true light. As due reward, the selfless sharer is always refilled with more and better from the divine largesse. The all-encompassing wisdom of God is beyond bounds and limits. Mortal man is only able to scratch the surface. Man's knowledge and experience with the Divine is ever unfolding. He that walks in true faithfulness with God will have a lifetime of amazing discoveries to uncover and unending experiences to testify about.

Of great importance and never to be overlooked is the fact that there are three dimensions of the Divine. In order for the believer to experience the Divine fully, it is necessary that he grows in three distinct areas of faith. The first is the area of the spirit which calls all believers to seek after God first before the things of the world take deep root to tie them down. All men can and do have experience with some measure of the spirit of the Divine. It comes in trickles as the voice of the conscience within that urges mankind to live by Truth and love others as he would himself. It flows in the faithful believer as the power that enables him to do the amazing to God's glory.

The second is the area of the knowledge and fulfillment of God's promises to man. The fulfillment of God's promises can be experienced through grace as the believer learns and lives in accordance with the teachings of Christ. Most believers are stuck in the second area which is the realm of grace and never grow beyond it. They are stuck there because it is the material benefit of grace that motivates them and not true love for Christ or the heavenly way. These are the ones who obtain the rewards but not the blessing that come with faith in God through Christ.

The seekers after rewards hoard material possessions along the way but are denied salvation and eternal life with the heavenly Father. They may have some measure of the divine experience through Christ but will never know fully to be received by the heavenly Father as sons. The third area of spiritual growth is that of knowledge of the heavenly Father which can only be experienced by the few who partake worthily of grace and grow in faith to stand upright before God in mercy. It is for such that the Holy Ghost is given to inform and the Holy Spirit to enable mightily. They receive all gifts with thankfulness to God and never fail to share what they receive with others in charity as love urges them.

Peace within and contentment without is the hallmark of the sharers and proof of their worthiness in grace. Because the worthy come in true love and not for gain, they duly grow to full spiritual maturity in Christ to be received by the Father as sons. Such are the ones given the passport of life to become the brethren of the Christ or 'Christ-Men' and divinely ordained to change humanity for better. They receive eternity's irreversible gift because they have passed judgment and proven to be real in the crucible of Christ. Such are the ones given to have the key of greater understanding and due access to Providence.

The season of judgment or self-examination within the fellowship of Christ serves faithful believers well. It helps to move them from the spiritual indolence of grace on to the spiritual vitality of mercy. Granted that not every believer has been ordained to come into the realm of mercy, it is important to note however that no one who truly desires a place therein is left behind. The unworthy that is stuck in grace is the goat that hides among the sheep of the flock to defile the divine feast of grace in greedy lust. The goats in the sheepfold always stick out when the rug of grace is removed. The unfaithful fall when the rug of grace is pulled back for there is no place left to hide under judgment but the faithful are left standing to bask in new knowledge and vision about God.

Chapter Notes

- ✓ There is a morning appointed for the true believer when he will see and know all things in a new light.
- ✓ There is always a son ordained to receive from the future and another to keep the past at bay.
- ✓ Hearts that are joined as one in love by Truth turn human weaknesses into marvelous strength.
- ✓ The matured in Spirit can have much accomplished for he has the help of a host of divine messengers.
- ✓ Spiritual rebirth must come about before man can come into the love and knowledge of the Divine.
- ✓ Peace within and contentment of soul without is a divine birthright and affirm spiritual worthiness.
- ✓ Total spiritual transformation courses through the indolence of grace on to the vitality of mercy.
- ✓ There is no hiding place under the judgment of light when the rug of grace is lifted.
- ✓ The faithful that passes judgment basks in the light of new knowledge and vision about God.

It evokes a divine sunshine

That makes darkness to flee

When hearts are joined as one

As flames fused through love

Chapter 3

FOR THE PURE OF HEART

The kingdom of God is the realm where the validity of God's promises is verified and its promises fully realized. Therein all things can be known but one can only know as one is known. It is a world that reveals itself to the pure of heart that live by Truth. But on the other hand, it conceals itself from those hearts wherein darkness still lurks. Put simply, it is a mirror that best reflects the man that resides within each person. The purer that man's heart becomes is the clearer that man's spiritual vision gets so that he can truly begin to 'see' the self within, the world around him as well as the world beyond as should.

The best reference point or marker for Truth is the man within each person or his 'spirit-man'. Everything else extends from that point and can reach the utmost or zenith where the Divine can be joined by the very pure of heart. But where darkness resides in the heart, then the man within is blinded and can only see within a darkened veil or in shadows. In that case, the point of reference that extends from within can only reach a little distance upwards before arching back downwards to the earth. The impure of heart can only see to the point of his nose so to say unlike the pure of heart that can see up to the horizon and beyond. The kingdom of God is manifested in Truth and by purity of heart. It is clearly perceived by the pure of heart for such can ascend in spirit to be availed a heavenly perspective. But the impure of heart is a soul soon shrouded in darkness to become the short-sighted. Such soon lies down in the world to be deemed unclean by the Divine. The spirit that is lifted up into the kingdom of God is one fit to be acceptable as 'holy' on to the Divine.

The kingdom of the world is indeed a place where angels tread lightly for it portends death and destruction to the unwary. It is a place that takes the soul prisoner and binds the spirit of the faithless to the earthen to keep him estranged from God. The kingdom of the world is a subterfuge for man's flesh whereas the kingdom of God is a place of exalted refuge for his spirit. There is a clear and marked distinction between the two. One life is lived for the flourishing of the spirit on to eternity with God but the other is lived for consumption by the flesh on to spiritual death. The faithful believer that lives in the kingdom of God is led on the path of righteousness in all his endeavors and all who follow after him will be led along the same path. There is no risk of being lost in the world for all who walk with the righteous.

The spirit of the world, that is the unclean, will always yield to the Divine spirit wherever encountered. But the unclean spirit will not yield to the spirit that is infirm, uncertain and mixed up in its ways. The believer must choose one or the other in order to be counted on the side for which victory over the world has been divinely appointed. He that choses Truth and is pure of heart can receive the full benefits of the kingdom of God. But he is called to disavow and disassociate from the ways of the world in order to be deemed worthy to receive.

For the believer to walk and remain on the path of righteousness in a world that is mixed up, he must become accustomed to calling on God daily through prayers to lead and guide his footsteps. Praying through the day helps the believer to stay connected to the Divine Father. It is through prayers that mankind is tuned to hear the heavenly tweets or beacons of hope that guide the steps of the faithful. Prayer, diligent study, and meditation on the word of God work together to help the faithful believer take every step as well as do all things in the light of better understanding. Such whose steps are guided in the light will be spared from the stumbles and missteps that bedevil many in today's world. The guided no longer strives in his own might for he has learned to rely on God's help. He has learned that he can do much better and accomplish much more in the spirit of the living God who now accompanies him through the earthly journey.

The believer that keeps company with God can do the seemingly impossible or such works that shine to elicit praise for God from men. He is called to live in the humility that reserves praise for the Creator and not the creature so that he can be divinely exalted to receive due honor in the fullness of time. The humble in spirit will always answer when God calls him to Heaven's delight. Even though such asks for only little yet life offers him much good anyway. Goodness becomes the allotment of the man led by the spirit of love for he will be favored by the heavenly Father with all of life's blessings. In effect, such is an intrepid traveler or a universal spirit who will always find safe harbor and victory along life's journey for the heavenly Father will never leave or forsake him.

It is well noted that God's day begins at dusk and breaks in dawn. This is indeed true in that the Divine reaches out in mercy to the true believer when his footsteps stumble and he is down on his 'luck' so to say. The Spirit of God comes to lead the seeker through the night time of life so that he can break through in dawn at the end. It may take longer than expected but morning is always the outcome of faithfulness. Every journey on which the believer embarks must be taken faithfully to its conclusive end. There is no other way for the believer to be shed with God's glory unless he is willing to trust and follow God all the way. The end of the journey is always the place promised by the heavenly Father for he never fails to deliver. God always does things the right way and oftentimes that way turns out to be the long way less travelled. The divine way is never to hurry or waste but to do the marvelous to behold in patient love that never disappoints. Without a doubt, God always comes through to deliver as promised indeed at the end. The path on which the Spirit of God leads is often not understood nor the one expected by mankind but it always works out for the best in the end. Oftentimes, it is a path that leads through a maze but it always comes out at the place promised. The amazing God leads through a maze in order to get the believer there in the best way and time possible. The time spent in the maze serves to teach enduring lessons and prepare the trusting for what God has planned for him ahead.

The maze through which God leads mankind is indeed a path of amazement. The faithful believer simply has to trust and obey. He must cultivate the habits of singing and praying even when things seem not to be going well. He must never cease from giving thanks to God for redemption and life's blessings both little or grand. The thankful heart will always be the joyful heart that God will never turn his back on. It sounds simple enough but regrettably many take life's gifts for granted and fail to be thankful to God as due. The lack of due thankfulness to the heavenly Father lead many to have weak faith. Sadly, weak faith makes for the infirm spirit which rolls over in the dust of the world easily when difficulties are encountered.

For the strong of faith, there is an inaudible voice loud enough for the tuned heart to hear that guides mankind through life's journey. It is best heard in contemplative solitude and moments of disassociation from an invasive world. For this reason, the life lived in meditative and quiet peace most often leads to a deeper intimacy with God. It is in moments of meditative contemplation when he takes a little break from the world that the faithful believer finds his bearings and is revived in spirit to go the next mile. This kind of spiritual retreat is highly necessary and mostly needed by the true believer from time to time. The faithful believer is like a rechargeable battery energized by the power of the spirit of God. He is discharged as he carries out the earthly duties that so please the heavenly Father. Therefore he must seek out time in order to become recharged for the next duty cycle. This ebb and flow is a constant theme of spiritual life and echoes the refrain of renewal. Mankind has to take a break ever so often so that the spirit, mind and body can remain in harmony and ever ready to serve God as called.

The fully matured in Christ are indispensable warriors in God's kingdom. God wills and acts through them to effect comprehensive changes as his tentacles among humanity For all intents and purposes, they see, hear, taste, feel, speak, go as well as carry out countless other tasks for God on earth. God is never seen with the eyes of the flesh but it is by the fully matured in Christ that many come closest to catch a glimpse of the Divine in that they are given to manifest Godly attributes. It is helpful to think of the fully matured in Christ as a sort of messenger being put to various actions by the unseen hand of God. But the faithful willingly yields to God's impulses and directives out of love and not by coercion.

This is the big difference for God will not force mankind but gives everyone the freedom to obey or disobey him. This is what defines faith and frames new life through Christ. Simply put, faith is a relationship where the believer yields his will to be 'manipulated' by God to achieve his grand designs on earth. Regrettably, very rarely do the followers after Christ totally yield for God to lead in every area of life. There is always the human tendency to hedge or hold back in some areas. It is that way because mankind often thinks that he can do better in those areas by himself. In consequence, most of those who profess the name of Christ come in various degrees and measures of faith. Strong faith which defines full maturity in Christ is a rare occurrence. It can never happen without the approval and acknowledgment of the heavenly Father himself. It is reserved for the souls that God chooses to keep for eternal habitation with him as elect sons. It is only to such that he assigns new names.

There is a curious phenomenon that takes place when God elects a son. The world will mystifyingly turn on him. The elect of God is never well received but rather blamed for all that troubles the land. It is through this mystifying process of making him an escape goat in the world's eyes that the sacrificial lamb in God's eye is elected and appointed for divinity. It is the way up through being down. It is being poor so as to inherit the earth. It is dying in dust's shame so as to rise in light's glory.

In due time, the elect one that was once reproached comes to be the cornerstone of the building. He is always the leper rejected to be sought after by all in the appointed time and season of glory. The outsider is a friend of lepers for he is one himself. He is the guiltless one who must demonstrate divine love for all by paying for the sins of the guilty. He will suffer the leprosy laid on him by the sins of others for a season. But through him the sins of many will be forgiven so that they too will come to have a new vision of God. It is in this way that the sons live to secure the future from the sins of the past. They live to demonstrate how the mistake of Adam can be erased through the retake of Christ. Each son is a sacrificial lamb acceptable to God by whom many come into new life and reconciliation with the heavenly Father.

Chapter Notes

- ✓ The kingdom of God is a realm revealed to the pure of heart but concealed wherein darkness lurks.
- ✓ The kingdom of the world portends death for it entraps the soul in the earthen.
- ✓ The spirit of uncertainty will yield when confronted by that of certainty in the spiritual scheme.
- ✓ The Spirit of God leads through the night time in order for man to wake up in a fulfilling dawn.
- ✓ The path on which the divine Spirit leads man is a maze but it works out best in the long run.
- ✓ The still small voice of God is best heard in moments of contemplation away from the worldly.
- ✓ The fully matured is spirit can travel in light anywhere and anytime as uplifted by the Divine.
- ✓ The fully matured in spirit is often well-received everywhere but a stranger among his own folk.
- ✓ The faithful that endures suffering for love soon becomes inextricably bound with the Divine.
- ✓ The pure of heart travel on the golden strand where heaven and earth meet.
- ✓ The believer that willingly suffers for the sins of others is duly anointed as God's earthly helper.

Counsel for vainglorious appetites

Let the unwary take good note

Promises to deliver much for little

Always end up as good for nothing

Chapter 4

STILL SMALL NUGGETS

All who faithfully walk in divine light are often battered and bruised by the assault of a world that rejects them as contrarians. But through those assaults come a renewal in mind as well as growth in spirit that leads into a fuller and deeper understanding of God's ways. Such situations and circumstances encountered along the way, no matter how unpleasant they may have been, serve as permanent markers to define all who truly seek after divine light and add up to a baptism of fire in the spirit of Truth. It is this roasting in the fire of the spirit that leaves an indelible mark and identifies the faithful as belonging to God.

In order to become matured in Christ, the faithful must carry the deep wounds of suffering and crucifixion inflicted by the world for love of Truth. Though the journey to spiritual maturation is a harrowing challenge, it is the process by which the old self is buried so that a far better new self can come forth. It is the spiritual climb up the mountain of faith that leads to heaven's tableland. He that reaches that mountain top will become changed forever in that he has overcome the world. He has joined the living church which constitutes the reborn in spirit or christened in light. He has become one bestowed with great vision and strong faith who can receive all things that he wishes from God in mercy. He is one given to receive the full anointing that is the irreversible gift of Christ.

No one is able to make it to receive the full anointing and be christened in light unless it is given to him to do so by the heavenly Father. It takes the Spirit of God to will and act within the believer to sustain him as he labors upwards in faith. The divine spirit sustains the believer when he has written the laws of God in the tablet of his heart and lives in accordance with the Truth therein. It is by faithful obedience to Truth that the seeker becomes established in faith to no longer walk alone but in the congregation of those being perfected through Christ.

The faithful believer that walks in that congregation is a vessel prepared to receive heavenly gifts from the Divine to share with the needy. He is one found worthy in God's eye to not only receive gifts but to offer up prayers and make petitions on behalf of others. However he must walk on the 'strait' and narrow path of righteousness in order to remain a vessel fit for worthy service. He must remain righteous and hold the things entrusted to his care in good custody so that God and not man is duly glorified. The love of God and the fear of displeasing him is the starting point where man begins to intermeddle with divine wisdom. Wisdom involves prescient knowledge that duly appears as needed. It is informed knowledge that helps mankind deal with the issues of the day as such appear along life's path. The words of wisdom are always fitly spoken for they address the core issues within every problem and provide insightful solutions where none had seemed to exist. Wisdom can be understood as that insightful knowledge and good information that seems to appear out of the wellspring of the mind at a moment's notice when needed. It is one way in which the heavenly Father reassures his own that he is with them always.

Often times God entrusts the faithful believer with hidden knowledge and uncommon insight. This is knowledge that God makes available on a need to know basis. These streams of enlightenment often deal with certain truths that have not been clearly understood before. Also as man's horizon widens and his level of understanding deepens, the Father opens up new veins of golden truths for him to mine. It is through this process that God progressively leads the faithful into a better understanding of his ways. It is in this light that man is spiritually remade in the divine image to come into full knowledge of God.

The faithful believer that has come into the full knowledge

of God has joined up with the Divine. Such has become an enlightened soul that intermediates in spirit between the heavenly and the earthly. He is like an alternator that charges up those willing to embrace Truth with the essence of the Spirit from above. It is by affording them this spiritual jump-start that many come into knowledge of the Divine and into the everlasting. Such that have full knowledge of God are certain of faith and will dutifully obey his commands so that the divine plan for humanity may come to pass. The heavenly Father affords prescient knowledge and sparks of divine wisdom to aid the faithful and protect him in an unscrupulous world. It is this informed knowledge that equips those faithful in the way of Christ to be wise as the serpent but gentle as a dove as they carry about in the world.

The kingdom of the world is a spiritual wasteland where men sacrifice their souls for the pursuit of earthly materials and selfish gain. It is not a place of the easy yoke but a place that is very taxing on mankind's soul both individually and collectively. It is not a desirable place for the believer who seeks after God and deems his soul to be precious above the fleeting and transitory. The believer who deems his soul to be precious knows that he is only a sojourner and stranger in the world who is called to pass through it in a certain way. The heavenly Father is aware of his predicament as a stranger in the world and makes provision in advance for him along life's path so that his soul is never compromised. But the faithful must never transgress the laws so as to remain on the righteous path that he knows to be true or he will miss out on those things that God has prepared for him along the way.

The faithful believer has to trust and walk in the direction that God leads. He will find that a table is always prepared for him but he must be perceptive in spirit in order to receive what has been prepared in the way. He cannot be double-minded but must remain certain in faith and unwavering in his devotion. Dutiful prayer and worship allows him to be anchored in peace, so that he can continue to hear the whispers of the voice of Truth that speaks to him. Within the inaudible whispers of that voice lie the seed of his blessing for the day and seed-thoughts or memos for the good works ordained for him.

The mercies of God are tendered in sprinkles as the golden showers of divine blessing. Mercy does not come in a deluge but in sufficient quantity to meet the needs of the day and season. It has to be that way so that it can be accommodated without much trouble and well managed when received. The faithful believer must know how not to offend the spirit and thereby close the door to Heaven's blessings. The door of mercy is always open for the faithful deemed worthy by God. The whole creation is given to aid such a believer in mercy for he exists in spiritual symbiosis with all living things. He is given to sustain all good things which will in turn sustain him in kind. It is by this spiritual symbiosis, where the faithful in Christ takes as needed but gives back as due, that he is woven into the fabric of life to be joined with the ever-lasting. It is in this way that the faithful duly become nodes of creation and extensions of the Divine on earth.

There is information and then there is noise. Not all information is useable and useful. Information and knowledge that is of no benefit clutters the mind and lends weariness to the flesh. Informed knowledge is highly beneficial and desirable for victorious living. The Spirit of God speaks to the heart in a still small voice but the spirit of world shrieks and shouts noisily. It floods and deluges the mind with more than it can process. It is ceaseless in besieging the mind to make one flawed choice after another. If this choice does not suit the fancy then the other will surely do it. If the sour does not suit one's taste then the sweeter will definitely satisfy the palate. It is all just beguiling fluff that promises fulfillment but only delivers emptiness. The spirit of the world is like the conniving used car salesman that saddles the unwary buyer with that damaged but prettied up vehicle that he does not need nor can ill afford. It is all wanting, hasting and wasting that feeds the vain glorious appetite with the fake to leave him with an empty feeling afterwards.

The still small voice of the spirit of God speaks to the

needful and enduring things that bring fulfillment in life. It reasons with the spark of goodness in man to consider his ways and choose the right path. He that yields to the direction of the guiding voice of Truth will find fulfillment and produces good fruits as due. Good outcomes crown the endeavors of such who obey in faith. The voice of Truth need not shout to be heard for it is heard in the heart. It is heard and known by the heart that seeks to know in light. It is not heard by the empty heart that seeks after the worldly. It is heard by those who trust and believe that God is ever in control. The heart that embraces the still small voice in good hope progresses into the greater light of understanding but he that rejects 'Him' regresses further into darkness.

Much is heard and understood by those hearts that welcome and accommodate Truth through Christ. Such are the valiant few who dare to stand tall regardless of cost. They live in truth and yield in total obedience to the divine will. Such are led into the kingdom of God in due season wherein all things glow in the light of truth and love. Therein all tarry in hope for it is not a place for those who run in their own will but for those who have learned to wait on God. The work ordained therein is accomplished with patience for the enduring are not rushed but carried out in purposeful order in accordance with divine will.

The place of hope and good expectations that the Spirit of

the Father leads the trusting believer to is Ephraim. He is the little one that God showers with tender mercies. The place of Ephraim is a seed of the Divine. It is a node of the creative impulse that brings out new things out of the old. It is the place of the little seed that has the potential to produce great things. The seed of Ephraim has been set aside by God for the beloved few who have opted to choose him over the world. Such may start with nothing but will be afforded the ingredients to accomplish much through God's love. The faithful believer that has been led into Ephraim must learn to choose wisely for all that he wishes for will be granted. It is a place for the humble in spirit where there is no need for the praise of men. Therein all things are done in the power of the spirit of the living God and for his divine glory. Ephraim may begin as that little place on the edge of the wilderness but it duly increases to abound in great hope.

Chapter Notes

- ✓ Broiling in the fire of the Spirit permanently marks the faithful believer as one who belongs to God.
- ✓ The faithful able to ascend faith-mountain has overcome the world and is changed forever.
- ✓ Only the righteous that hold God's precious things in good custody are able to scale faith-mountain.
- ✓ God opens up new veins of golden truths for the faithful to mine as his understanding deepens.
- ✓ Every son is an enlightened soul that intermediates in spirit between the earthly and heavenly.
- ✓ The kingdom of the world is not a desirable place for the man that values his soul as precious.
- ✓ The faithful that walk in the way that the divine Spirit leads find a table prepared before them.
- ✓ The tender mercies do not come in a deluge but in good measure to meet the need of the day.
- ✓ Informed knowledge does not clutter the mind but is focused and directed at the heart of the matter.

Mercy seeks in hope and rewards with life

For without it death roams about freely

It is the sunshine that warms the heart

As well the dew that waters thirsty souls

Chapter 5

FROM PERCH OF MERCY

God is not enamored with the many that pay him lip service by professing his name loudly. Rather his delight is to seek after the few who confess and serve him sincerely out of a pure heart. The spirit of God does not dwell in the noisome places where mankind often gathers to clamor for attention but rather in the quiet and peaceable places where man's heart is focused on him. A garden is a good representation of that quiet and peaceable place. A garden is where the divine purposes proceed in orderly conduct and nature displays herself in a lovely showcase. It is an ideal place for man to learn the unhurried directed pace of the divine way. A garden is devoid of the noisy interferences that often make it difficult for mankind to meditate and digest the meat of Truth.

The milk of the word of God is for the new and young beginner in the way of Christ. But to grow into spiritual maturity in light, the believer must be able to eat and digest the meat of Truth. Therefore a time comes in the spiritual life of the young believer, when he must become a man of faith. That time will never come unless he is able to put away childish things. The young in faith that is not able to tune out and turn off childish impulses will remain a believer in name only. He will never have faith that is rooted in experience with the Divine. Such can be easily misled for he is not anchored on the solid rock of the Almighty. Rather he will be given to look for the light of Christ everywhere except within himself. He will inevitably end either as an uncertain believer transfixed in fear or the non-believer that stampedes through life in hurried stumbling steps.

The believer who has grown from milk to eat and digest the meat of the word is the man of faith given to dwell on the spiritual housetop. The latter is for those who have been able to let go of the world so as to ascend upwards in spirit. It is from the vantage point of that housetop that the believer can be focused on God and availed due knowledge. It is from there that the believer is able to perceive that which is beyond the horizon to become a discerner of the future and the harbinger of the new. Because of his unique perspective, the dweller on the spiritual housetop is an agent of transformation who can change the human landscape for better. The spiritual housetop is the perch of mercy from which the good shepherd watches out dutifully for the sheep of the flock.

The spiritual housetop is a platform for prophecy from which things that loom on the horizon and lurk around the corner can be known. For that reason, the spiritual housetop is a desirable place for the believer to aspire for and to remain once up there. He who dwells there in spirit must not come down for he is one in communion with the Divine. He may be in the world but he is no longer of it. Rather all things that are in the house, that is to say the bottom dwellers mired in earthiness, must aspire to rise and join the spiritual dweller on the housetop.

All who dwell below and aspire for the spiritual housetop must not be concerned with the reproach of the world. It takes the battering and bruising that the world directs at the believer to dislodge the encumbering mud cake of the past that weighs down the spirit. The world's reproach is the toll that must be paid so that the spirit within can be free to ascend higher. It is a small token when compared to a future to be spent in company of the Divine as well as the goodness and mercy that comes to attend the ascendant spirit. It is the token that has to be paid to cross the bridge of destiny and escape from the tethers of the world into the freedom of hope. All believers must strive to ascend to the spiritual housetop for thereon can be found the only safe refuge from the overwhelming flood of malaise that unceasingly threatens to engulf mankind.

The faithful must cross the bridge of destiny in order to

escape the overwhelming dismal flood that licks at humanity's doorsteps. He must cross the bridge bearing his cross on his back. He may have to crawl on his hands and knees to get over that bridge in order to find refuge. He must cross the bridge for beyond it await safety and redemption. He that crosses the bridge will find the secure place of faith-rest where life is lived in penitent humility to God's glory, praise and honor. He that has found a place on the housetop is one justified before God. He is one called to receive from above and to share with those below so that they too may come to be lifted up as well.

He that dwells on the housetop is the bearer of messages that are too important to be withheld from humanity or compromised by the unfaithful. He is the voice of hope for the future through which salvation cries out. He is the last responder sent to the lost and floundering soul earmarked for redemption. He is given to speak Truth with an urgency that is often met with disbelieving indifference. Yet such is one who carries on for God and humanity though burdened by his duty nevertheless. The praise of mankind and the material benefits which can be gained from men is not the motivation for him. Rather he knows that the approval and love of the heavenly Father is a far better blessing to be desired above what the world offers.

The message of hope for mankind through Christ is too important not to be delivered and the Truth too revelatory not to be told. Most who profess to walk in light prefer the milk of the word. But no matter how sincere the milk, it is purposed to enable new born babies grow in the season of spiritual infancy. It takes the meat of the word to mature into the man of God. Spiritual babies reproduce babies after themselves but the spiritual man produces a son after God.

The truth about the demands of the way that leads to spiritual maturity is displeasing to most ears and hard to swallow for many. Therefore the Truth is often watered down for men's liking and mass appeal. It is in so doing that the purity of the message of the light of Christ becomes blunted so that many have come to be left in an arrested spiritual development. The true gospel is meat and the watered down is milk. The believer who is left in an arrested spiritual development is fearful, doubtful and unable to rise to the spiritual housetop. He will not mount up with the wings of the eagle for he will lack requisite faith. He will lack the spiritual strength and fortitude to forge ahead when trouble appears on the way. He will be one not given great vision and strong faith.

The faithful who is able to eat and digest the meat of the word is one that becomes duly matured in Christ. He will become transformed soon enough into a spiritual image of the Divine to become a member among those reborn in the light of Christ. But none of this can take place unless there is forgiveness of sins. Forgiveness of sins can only be obtained through the justification of God and it is for the believer willing to let go of all hurts and injustice rendered to him by men to receive. It is for this reason that wisdom declares that blessed are the merciful for they shall obtain mercy. The faithful that are justified before God become adopted into the divine household under mercy as the reborn in light whose sins are remembered no more.

Where forgiveness of sins has been obtained, the guilt of past sins no longer exists. There is a release and freedom of spirit that is experienced from the dissolution of guilt. It brings with it a new found peace that not only fosters the awakening but the flourishing of new life. It invigorates the spirit so that it can rise upwards to the utmost of the heavenly realm. It can be said then that the believer has become the faithful fitted with the wings of the eagle in divine glory. To be fitted and mounted up with the wings of the eagle affords the faithful believer the spiritual updraft to lift him up into the realm of mercy. In that realm all things can be known, can be obtained and can be sustained for mercy is comprehensive indeed.

He that dwells under mercy is able to stand before God for he has become known by the Father. He that can stand before God has become exalted in spirit and is privy to conversations in heavenly places as one given to serve divine purposes on earth. The faithful that is joined with

Divine in spirit must focus on the high and lofty things for the heavenly Father will grant his wishes duly. He will be given to ride upon the high places of the earth with the fullness of the blessings of Israel always at hand to attend his way. He will find that provision has been made along every path that he walks and that he will always have the knowledge as well as the wisdom necessary to produce pleasing outcomes always.

The wisdom that the merciful are bestowed with helps to heal the sick, make the wounded whole, repair the broken, refresh the thirsty and restore the dying. It is wisdom that is capable of endless wonders and such amazing works that make men give God due glory. The works accomplished when mankind is joined with the Divine shine so that the great power of God may be witnessed by all. It is with such divinely availed wisdom that the faithful becomes a breaker of new grounds given to do things in new ways that have never been done before. Such handiworks directed by the unseen guiding hand of divine wisdom may be likened to the honey comb that is sweet and fulfilling to the souls of men.

As mentioned earlier, he that must accomplish such works must remain on the spiritual housetop so that his mind can remain focused on the high things that bring glory to God and not be concerned with the worldly. The divinely inspired works that shine before men are done in the valley but the wisdom to do them comes from above. The faithful receive from exalted places in light in order to share with other men in the valley below in love. He that is grafted to share divine wisdom in this wise is in effect one that walks as Heaven's emissary among men. All who are such dwell in a place secure within the kingdom of God where they are immune from the evil in the world.

The kingdom of God is the new land fixed and secure where the way of light is the foundation. The kingdom of the world on the other hand is a turbulent sea of darkness that froths with uncertainty and wanton anger. Its foundation shifts with unexpected twists and turns that leave the misguided dazed with disappointed hopes. There are different and opposite sensibilities to living in either the kingdom of God or that of the world. The dwellers in the kingdom of God are guided in spirit to demonstrate the way of life within the divine fold. All such have been established under the mercy of God to live as model vessels chosen to exemplify kingdom life in the love and light of Christ. It is for this reason that they travel calmly on life's road for they have the assurance of spirit that all will be well for them through the earthly journey.

The kingdom of God is a place of demonstrating the power in the Truth that had been taught and received by the faithful at heart. It is a realm reserved for those who have received such Truth in good faith and live in accordance with its teaching. Such who dwell in this spiritual realm will begin to access the power of God to much effect. They will begin to appropriate a host of services through the Spirit of the most-high God. The faithful who have entered into that realm have ceased from laboring alone. All such handiworks that are ascribed to them are done through the power of the spirit of God. In that realm, all things are done in the greater light that precludes wanting, hurrying and wasting. All who dwell there are the good custodians who have learned to maintain what has been entrusted into their care with due diligence. Such take what is needed, use it for fruitful purposes and replace same in good stead so that all who are of good faith may share in its benefits to the glory of God.

To dwell in the kingdom of God is to live in the place of the endless cycle of divine blessing. It is the life lived where the guiding standards are according to the pattern and orderliness of heaven. For the faithful believer to be the good custodian who maintains what has been entrusted to him in diligent care, he has to be washed in soul and broiled in the fire of the spirit of Truth through Christ. The process of washing the soul prepares the faithful so that he can grow from grace unto mercy. The washing of the soul results from the material and personal choices made by the believer as he seeks after a reconnection with the Divine. The material and personal sacrifices made by the believer as he chooses God over the world serve to reset his mind towards God and pare down the contents of the earthly backpack that he carries to the bare essentials in order to streamline his life. Such streamlining helps to prepare and condition the mind and flesh so that man's spirit can focus better on the heavenly.

The washing of the soul works as an amplifier in the life of the believer so that the still small guiding voice of God can be clearly and loudly heard. It helps to bring the faithful to the doorstep of the Divine. The faithful must be willing to enter through that door and take a seat. He must be willing to commend his spirit into divine safe keeping and let God's will be done in his life. He must be willing to trust and join his will to that of the divine Father. He can never do better otherwise or get a better deal elsewhere. To enter through the door that separates from the worldly is the grand decision of faith. It is the choice that must be made if the believer desires to come into an everlasting bond with the heavenly Father. To enter through the door is to go all the way to full maturity in Christ so that the mortal can become the immortal remade in divine image.

Chapter Notes

- ✓ It is from the perch of the spiritual housetop that the eye of the spirit can be truly focused on God.
- ✓ The encumbering mud cake of the past has to be dislodged and washed off before the spirit can rise.
- ✓ The faithful that has received justification can petition and receive forgiveness for others that ask.
- ✓ There is a release and freedom of spirit obtained from the dissolution of guilt that fosters new life.
- ✓ The faithful that are joined with the Divine will be privy to conversations in heavenly places.
- ✓ The kingdom of the world shifts with twists and turns that leave many with disappointed hopes.
- ✓ The kingdom of God is a place that validates the power of the truth laden in the faithful heart.
- ✓ The 'shame of the cross' is the payment that declares that mankind has given his heart to God.
- ✓ The faithful divine vessel labors under the obscured self so that God may have the glory.
- ✓ The reborn in light is given to re-create the old where the new is always better than the former.

Prescient knowledge and wisdom

As living water from the Divine

Issue forth from mercy's throne

For the sons to receive and share

Chapter 6

URGE TO RE-CREATE

Wisdom declares in Truth that God is the Creator of Heaven and earth as well as all things contained therein. Mankind must never be deluded into thinking otherwise. All things in creation originated from God's all-knowing mind and came into being by his divine motive and impulse. It is the same mind that the heavenly Father avails to all who come to full spiritual maturity through Christ. All who have been availed such minds are the reborn or christened in light adopted as sons of Heaven. The sons are all like cookies that have been baked in the same mold. The coloring may vary but the ingredients in the baking mixture are the same for the essence of the Divine remains the same yesterday, today and forever.

The heavenly Father uses the sons to carry out his divine purposes on earth and bring about such works that shine to bring him due glory. It is the same mind and motif that created the grand universe that works to enable the sons to re-create their little plots on earth into a garden after the order of things in heaven. It is the same spirit that created the grand that is at work in them to create the little in faithful facsimile with the divine aesthetic. The mind, pattern and motif are similar but differ only in scale. A static discharge or little trickle of electricity is the same as the bolt of lightning that blazes across the sky or the megawatts of electrical power being generated by the grand generators of this age. It is the same consciousness stepped up to do great things or stepped down to do the little. The difference is only in the magnitude and scale of application.

The faithful believer who has been washed and purified in the fire of Truth through Christ has been readied in mind and spirit to be connected with the Divine. He may not be consciously aware of it but his thought processes will begin to mirror that of the heavenly Father. His handiworks will become universal in its appeal for he has become one remade in the image of the heavenly Father. His earthly plot or surroundings may be small in comparison to the size of the universe but the same hand of wisdom that fashioned the grand universe though unseen also acts in him to fashion his surroundings. In effect, he has begun to live a life patterned after the heavenly and within the order of the saintly in spirit.

The heavenly Father uses all who are being perfected in

the saintly order to demonstrate the heavenly way so that mankind can have the fulfilling and enduring in life. Such serve as models being displayed in the divine showcase as guiding lights for other men to follow and be led into the kingdom of God. By watching them many will come to understand the way of light for they are used to translate the heavenly ways on earth. Oftentimes, the saintly is not easily welcomed and embraced by the spiritually ignorant for the taste of the new wine takes some time to be appreciated. Nevertheless, he that is called in this wise must not be a shrinking violet but stand for Truth in order to be counted in the congregation of the mighty before the heavenly Father. Such is one who has joined the ranks of those given to make the impossible with men become possible in the power of the living God through Christ.

The mission of translating heaven on earth entails an endless cycle of commuting in spirit between the heavenly realm and the earthly domain. The bearer of light ascends in spirit to the mountain top to soak up the dew of wisdom and refreshment from the rain bearing clouds that abide there. He returns to pour out the life sustaining water to the parched and thirsty souls in the valley below. Living water is prescient knowledge and wisdom that flows out of the heavenly throne that is much needed to bring about regeneration and sustain new life through Christ.

It is by this interaction through love of the earthly and the heavenly that the kingdom of God is spread and the tabernacle of the faithful bearer of light enlarged. When this enlargement begins in true measure, the bearer of living water often discovers to his delight that the Father makes provision in men and materials to assist his efforts for the ploughman never muzzles the mouth of the oxen.

The heavenly Father uses all kinds of men as helpers in his grand design on earth but he chooses and pairs them up in ways that best complement each other's strength. The order of pairings when studied carefully provides great insight into the operating principles of the kingdom of God. It all works ideally so that the whole is greater than the sum of the parts. In the divine consciousness and economy, all things are known for what they truly are, appropriately named and hence wisely used.

Take for instance, the pairing of the disciple Simon (Peter) with Andrew as they were assigned together by Christ Jesus. Simon is the one that readily hears the still small voice of God. He is the same as Peter the extroverted one with the daring and adventurous impulse who gets the big picture but not the details within the picture. It can be said of Simon (Peter) that he views life through a lens that is zoomed out. Andrew, on the other hand, is the introverted one who is not fixated on the big picture but notices every little detail within view. It can be said that Andrew views life through a zoomed in lens. Andrew, as his name points out, is the one not easily discouraged by adversity or obstacles but given to show manly courage and remain composed when the odds seem to be against him. Peter can see the prize but Andrew can see the steps that are needed to attain that prize. Simon and Andrew must then be paired so that by working together they ensure that God's commands will always be carried out to the desired outcome.

Next take the pairing of the disciple James with John as assigned by Christ Jesus. James, as his name tells, is the one who understands that God's way is progressive and revelatory. He knows that God is always doing something new to help man understand the divine way a little better. John, according to his name, is the one who understands that God is merciful and will make allowances for the mistakes of man as he learns to take heavenly steps. James and John must then be paired so that both can work together to ensure that the pilgrim that seeks after God never looks back or give up in the way but make forward progress. By working together, both speak to the fact that the believer that stumbles and falls down must get up to press on in light's upward way for God will forgive such.

Next take the pairing together of the disciple Phillip with Nathaniel (Bartholomew). Phillip is the one who will bring the true seeker out of darkness into light. Nathaniel is he who is honest and without guile. (Bartholomew is the one given as a gift of God to men). Bartholomew and Nathaniel are both the same in spirit for there is no misgiving or regrets with the gift of God. Phillip must then be paired with Nathaniel (Bartholomew) so that the mission of enlightenment must not be perverted for personal gain but for the glory of God who gives his light as a free gift to mankind.

The same pattern of shoring up strengths with weaknesses to forge the better continues with the pairing of Levi (Mathew) and Thomas. Levi is the one given to dedicate his life to serve man on behalf of God. (Mathew is the one who has left the pursuit and love of the materialistic to offer up self as a gift to mankind). Mathew and Levi are both the same in spirit. Thomas is the one who always reserves judgment and know that men are far from what they claim to be. He is one given to look things over carefully for he knows that the world is a predatory place where things are not often what they seem. Mathew (Levi) must then be paired with Thomas so that the laborer for God must be wise as the serpent but gentle as a dove. The pure of heart must be protected from a capricious world that often wreaks havoc and devours the trusting.

The same pattern of tempering iron with carbon to forge steel continues with the pairing of James (the son of Alphaeus) with Simon (Zelotes). James (the son of Alphaeus) is the one who understands that man must first yield to be fashioned by God in order to be the vessel fitted for good works. He knows that he must be willing to tarry for God to make known his sovereign will as he works out his divine plans over the affairs of mankind. To do otherwise is to run before God and risk failure. The uninformed mind, though he may be enthusiastic, will stumble for without the spirit of God as guide man is blind. Simon (Zelotes) is the one who hears the voice of God in his heart, has unbridled enthusiasm and unfailing zeal. James (the son of Alphaeus) must therefore be paired with Simon (Zelotes) because enthusiasm and informed readiness are the ingredients that combine to win the battles of life. He that is readily prepared and waits in patient hope will always be well-positioned to take advantage when the right opportunity shows up.

Last is the pairing of Judas (the son of Alphaeus) with Judas (Iscariot). This last pairing is a cautionary tale for man not to judge men only by what they say but also by what they do. Judas (the son of Alphaeus) is the faithful one that knows to sing God's praises. He is always thankful for life's blessings and has a good understanding of God's patient ways. Judas (Iscariot) is the one who also loves to sing praises but fails to understand God's ways for he thinks that his own way is better. He is the one who professes loudly but whose spirit is after material gain. These two men with the same name but clearly contrasting spiritual make-ups must therefore be paired together so that it can be made clear to all that at the end of the day when it matters most it is not what the believer says but what he does that counts most with God.

Based on these pairings, the operating principles of the kingdom of God can be understood within the following seven guidelines. Firstly, God assigns a new name to the man that he has chosen out of the world. Secondly, the still small voice of God's commands must always be obeyed to its conclusive end when heard by the believer. Thirdly, the believer will make forward progress if he never gives up in the face of challenges. Fourthly, the faithful believer must not labor for personal gain but for the glory of God. Fifthly, the faithful believer though he lives in an evil world is protected from its evils. Sixthly, the believer must remain ready in patient hope so that he will take his victory in its due season. Finally, it is not what the believer knows but what he does with what he knows that counts most with God. The operating principles listed above are the guidelines by which the new man of Christ progresses from victory to victory as he recreates heaven on earth.

Chapter Notes

- ✓ The same Spirit of God that created the universe is at work in the sons as they tend their earthly plots.
- ✓ The divine mind works in the faithful both to do the great and the little things that bring glory to God.
- ✓ The faithful that lives with a new vision of God translates the orderliness of heaven down to earth.
- ✓ The spiritually matured is a model displayed in a showcase so other men can learn about the Divine.
- ✓ All who labor to spread true light always find that God makes provisions to assist in the effort.
- ✓ God has a progressive nature and always looks for ways to help mankind understand him better.
- ✓ The operating principles of God's kingdom make the whole to be greater than the sum of the parts.
- ✓ God makes sure that the pure of heart that labors for love remains protected from evil in the world.
- ✓ The faithful must be prepared and wait in patient hope ready to serve the commanding will of God.
- ✓ The man reborn in light progresses to greater glory as he fulfills the urge to recreate heaven on earth.

For his works to be sublime

And shine brightly before all

The faithful must play a part

To help humanity see in light

Chapter 7

THE LIVING CHURCH

All who are reborn in divine light live to recreate heaven on earth as members of the living church of Christ. Such are the faithful who have ascended in spirit to the summit of God's mountain to come into an innumerable company of spiritual helpers. All who are members of this living church have joined with Christ Jesus in a commonwealth of the noble of soul and purified in spirit adopted by the heavenly Father to be extensions of his divine presence on earth. They are the ones within whose hearts the divine Father dwells and the flame of Calvary love burns.

The living church should never be confused with the earthly churches or temples of walls as it is a far different matter. The living church is not seen with the eyes of men but known in spirit. It is a congregation of those who have become members of the divine household. The heavenly Father chooses those worthy of such elect company and remakes them all in his image. The image is that of the reborn in divine light and wrought in the same unchanging spiritual mold through the ages. All who belong in that congregation constitute the true Israel and live to serve the divine will for they cannot do otherwise.

On the other hand, the role of the earthly churches or temples with walls has come to be greatly misunderstood in these times by many who are not better informed. The church with walls was only a platform for spreading the message of repentance onto salvation. It was a means of making sure that all men were aware of God's redemption plan for mankind through Christ. It was really a clearing house of information to help uninformed mankind understand that the way of the world was not the only of life but that there was another far better in the end.

Mankind can have that better life by reconciliation with his Creator in love through the path of truth and light after the footsteps of Christ Jesus. But first he has to let go of worldly ways and seek out God first before he can have the new life promised. It is only when man truly and faithfully follows that path that he can be transformed in spirit to join up with the Divine. There are no short-cuts and no easy way to be found on this path.

At its best, the earthly church was meant to provide a spring board from which the young believer can begin his faith journey as he embarks on a reunion with his Creator.

Sadly, the earthly church has become a place where many have been led to settle into an arrested spiritual development. Such begin the journey but are never able to attain full maturity in Christ because they have put their trust in men and institutions. The whole point of man's spiritual walk is to enable him to learn to put his trust in God who never disappoints and not on men or institutions for those do disappoint.

In its glory days of seasons long past, the earthly church spurred on by the Spirit of the living God was very effective in spreading the word about the way of light through Christ. It provided the impetus for many to reject the sinful ways of the world and be led back to the spiritual path on which the true living God is found. But along the way, the earthly church became opportunistic in exploiting the guilt of gullible many for the personal gain of the leadership. Over time the so-called leaders have proceeded to turn God's house into a market place and become much like evil shepherds who feed on the sheep of the flock.

It needs to be clarified that the leadership of men is purely technical for only the heavenly Father can be the leader of any church, institution or groups that invoke his name. God has long ceased from leading the earthly churches and temples but the Creator still loves man his beloved creation though fallen as he is. God will always love man for he is his favorite creation. The churches with walls have come to love the material more and God less. In effect, they have become culprits in the abuse of the gifts availed by God through grace.

It is a sad situation that has left God with no choice but to withdraw his right hand from among the earthly churches. It is not much different from the scenario that prompted the outrage of Christ Jesus at the wheelers and dealers at the temple in Jerusalem. The churches with walls have at best become institutions that cater to the social wants of men and not their spiritual needs. The true church of God is the living church without walls where the congregants are baptized in the spirit of Truth and perfected in love through Christ. It is not a physical but a spiritual church availed to the faithful as Heaven's tableland.

Put simply the earthly church of walls was meant to be a clearing house for information and not a place for spiritual settlement. Not only did the earthly church become a place of spiritual settlement for many but the glitter of silver and gold in its collection plates have dulled the pure light of the divine way therein. The earthly church has declined ethically to become presumptuous, compromise Truth, profane grace and over-reach its original mandate. It has misguidedly gone from seeking after the redemption of souls to seeking after gold. It has gone from a feast of charity to become a high priced restaurant with many offerings that hook the unwary with intoxicating chaff that bloats the flesh but suffocates the spirit. It long ago turned deaf ears to the heavenly mandate for man to prune the flesh so that the spirit within can flourish.

The earthly church was the original depository from which the seed of the gospel of Christ was planted in the world. The grain of Christ has been planted all over the world in many shades and variations to suit many tastes. The proliferation of the grain has also brought with it the flourishing of weeds and tares within the fellowship. The tares are the supposed believers that profess the message of Christ but are not true worshippers at heart. Consequently they will never experience full spiritual transformation and come to be reconciled with the heavenly Father. Such are the wolves in sheep's clothing that hide among the sheep fold. They are in the congregation for gain and not for love of God or the way of Christ. God has been patient to allow all that to take place for through the earthly churches he makes the worthy to find escape and find true light as due.

All earthly institutions, whether religious or secular, are subject to pollution, corruption, degradation and breakdown. There is a tendency for all earthly institutions to break down with the passage of time. It is the bane of man's existence on earth and overrides all his endeavors. Outside of divine intervention, all of man's endeavors are undertakings by which he shovels dead or dying things about from one place to another. It is only when the redemptive power of God is at work in his life that man's endeavors become sustainable, fulfilling and enduring.

The call for the return to the pure and true have always echoed down the ages as accounts of spiritual revivals bear witness. Some have always gotten the message and left the 'establishment' to journey on in faith in search of the truer and purer. Rejecting the ways of the world and the life of sin is a good start but the rendezvous with the Divine takes place on the spiritual journey and not in a building or earthly institution. Spiritual transformation and experience with the Divine takes place on the lonely walk of faith. It is on that path that the relationship with the divine is formed and forged.

The faithful that has been fully transformed in spirit has a compelling testimony that he must share with others. He must share so that the misinformed can come to know about the reality, faithfulness and abiding love of God. He starts with his immediate circle of family, friends and then on to others as he enlarges the tabernacle in accordance with divine urge. He is called to pour out the essence of godliness that he has been filled with as he deals with humanity so that others may come to know the Divine as well. Many will not receive Truth but those whom the heavenly Father has earmarked will do so in due season for he that has been transformed in spirit to manifest the attributes of godliness will invariably induce others to follow suit.

The lust after material possessions and worldly goods is a spiritual drag that has bound many to the earthy. It is a drag that prohibits the spirit from soaring into the exalted realm which is the congregation of the living church of Christ. Wisdom declares that it is easier for a camel to pass through the eye of a needle than for a rich man to enter into the kingdom of God. The believer who is able to love God above all the beguiling offerings of the world has overcome the mountain in the way. If he continues in true faithfulness and charity, he will go on to become a golden censer in spirit.

The golden censer or golden-hearted is one whose earthly sacrifices are pleasing to God. Such is a beloved vessel whose petitions and requests will be readily granted by God. The golden-hearted is one who has passed from the brazen who seeks after the praise of men to the humble in spirit who seeks after God's approval. He is one tuned in spirit to know what to pray for because the Holy Ghost will inform him as due. As such, he has become one given to pray for those things needed to transform humanity and make goodness to abound on earth.

Unfortunately the earthly church has approached the matter of grace the wrong way through the lust for material possessions and worldly goods. It has used the cover of grace to seek the kingdom of the world first before seeking that of God. It really should be about the kingdom of God first so that Providence can then feature prominently in mankind's daily affairs. In their misguidance and consequent blindness, many have excluded themselves from getting close to the mercy seat of the most high by the abuse of grace. The truth is that grace is transitional and serves to prepare the faithful believer for the greater availed through mercy. To be stuck in grace is to be starved of mercy.

Grace is for babies and adolescents in faith but mercy is for men of God matured in the way of light. The earthly church has become like the rich young man who professed to love God but could not come into the place close to the divine heart on account of his possessions. His attachment and overly emphasis on material possessions precluded him from coming into full spiritual maturity his good intentions notwithstanding. His heart was bound to the world's goods so that he could not have the goodness and fulfillment availed to mankind only by divine mercy.

The earthly church in its misguided 'understanding' is also like the prodigal son who has abused the grace of the Father in wasteful plunder. It is cause for great joy in Heaven that some have seen the light of Truth. These enlightened souls have escaped from the grips of the materialistic thrust that hides under the cloak of grace. They have escaped therefrom as 'Onesimus' to reach out for the knowledge of the fullness of the Father. Grace affords the faithful believer the preparation to enable him become established in faith so that he can stand before the heavenly Father in mercy. He that is stuck in grace will have his spirit come into arrested development. He will become a spiritual dwarf instead of the giant of faith that he could have been.

Spiritual dwarfism is the malaise that has led to the demise of the earthly church and temples of worship. He that is mired in an arrested spiritual development will remain in an intermediate stage and will never come to full spiritual maturity in the way of Christ. He will remain a brazen altar filled with the smoke of presumption instead of a golden censer emitting the fragrance of the offering well received by God. The fully matured in Christ is a golden censer whose ways are pleasing to God. God will no longer require sacrifice of him that gave all for love but demand mercy of him for blind humanity.

The appeal to the ignorant and uninformed is the same standard misinformation that has always bedeviled mankind. The misinformed has been deluded into thinking that material prosperity is sure proof indication that a man's way is pleasing to God. Nothing can be further from the truth. Material prosperity that is not tainted is welcome but it is a finite reward and not a blessing. A finite reward is constrained and limited in time as well as in place. Even the enemy of light, the prince of the darkness of this world, can give finite rewards but only God can bestow a blessing.

A blessing is grafted within the spirit of man but rewards are patched on to the flesh. There are no misgivings or regrets with a blessing but rewards are often taken for granted and misused. A reward is for a season and dries up soon enough but a blessing is an enduring gift that is generationally passed on to the worthy. God's blessing has many elements that extend to different areas of life. A blessing comes about when the spirit of God has been poured into the faithful believer so that goodness and mercy come to attend him always. A blessing is a binding covenant not limited by time or place. The truly blessed is a person of covenant who will always receive that which he prays for in that the Divine is at home in him. Such a blessed one is a divine talisman fashioned for victory through life's battles in much the same way that the ark of covenant was for ancient Israel.

Chapter Notes

- ✓ The role of the earthly church was to serve as a platform to spread the news of the way of Christ.
- ✓ God still loves humanity more than ever but his place of worship is men's hearts and not buildings.
- ✓ The glitter of silver and gold in the collection plates of earthly churches has dulled divine light there.
- ✓ The grain of Christ has been planted over the world in many shades and variations to suit all tastes.
- ✓ It is only when the redemptive power of God is at work that earthly endeavors become fulfilling.
- ✓ It is on the lonely walk of faith that the spirit is transformed and a relationship forged with God.
- ✓ The spiritually matured man is a golden censer fitted to offer up sweet smelling sacrifices to God.
- ✓ The professed believer settled in the earthly church will be hard-pressed to find the living church.
- ✓ The misinformed think that material prosperity is sure indication that a man's way is pleasing to God.
- ✓ God's blessings extend into many areas of life and follows the faithful at all times.

To go from darkness into light

Something has to be burned

It takes man's flesh and ego

To make the perfect fodder

Chapter 8

WITHIN THE DIVINE

He that is fully matured in Christ must resign himself to being rejected by not only unbelievers but by many professed believers as well. Most do not have the experience and will therefore not understand the life of the one that lives in full light. Such is often considered to be strange for he walks on the path less travelled and not on the well beaten tracks that many cluster on. He that walks in full light will have no place to lay down his head so to say for he will be under constant misunderstanding and attacks even among his very own. However he is called to be fully clothed in spiritual armor always so that he can always stand for Truth and light in unfailing love.

It is important that the faithful in the way never forget to pray for others in need even in the midst of his troubles and tribulations. The faithful that readily forgives and prays for others will have divine power at work in his life to help secure him victories. The believer that readily forgives others is soon established from grace on to mercy to enter into an intimate relationship with the heavenly Father. He will become adopted as a member of the divine household with a divine mandate to help bring the willing into the same place as he is. The members of the divine household are intimately connected in spirit with the heavenly Father. It is from the place of intimate connection that the spirit within becomes privy to divine will and the basis upon which the faithful believer walks through life with a blessed assurance.

A blessed assurance is realized by the believer when the Holy Ghost is availed. The latter brings needed knowledge and whispers encouragement to the matured believer. The Holy Ghost is the intimate means by which the heavenly Father communicates with the faithful believer. 'He' is the means by which the Father wraps his hand of love around the shoulder of the faithful as a gesture that says I will be with you always and will never leave or forsake you. Such is the means by which the Father affirms him who is exalted in spirit. The information borne of the Holy Ghost must never be disregarded or perverted for it is given from the mercy seat of God to be used wisely.

He that receives the gift of the Holy Ghost will have his perspective change from the earthly into the heavenly in that he will begin to see clearer and know much better. Such is indeed one who has joined the conversation in heavenly places. The knowledge borne of the Holy Ghost is imparted on a need-to-know basis and must always be put to use when received. The Holy Ghost comes to bear in the season when the believer has been established from grace on to mercy. 'He' comes to bear in the times when the believer is faced with a choice with no clear direction about how to proceed in life. He comes to console and show the way to a higher plane so that the faithful can find escape and be spared from being inundated or overwhelmed by prevailing circumstances.

The Holy Ghost always to come to bear in human experience at momentous times when a choice has to be made and an affirmation is needed. 'He' is given when some are chosen to step up to a higher purpose and greater calling. 'He' comes to separate the few out of the many originally called. 'He' comes to bear in humanity's defining moments and must never be disobeyed. The Holy Ghost is given to herald the beginning of a new era when the former has run its course in the life of the believer. The past counts little when the Holy Ghost comes to bear in the life of the faithful but the future counts much.

The Holy Ghost is given to affirm justification in the eyes of God. Offences committed prior to receiving the Holy Ghost are considered sins of ignorance but all transgressions committed after the Holy Ghost is given are offences that cannot go unpunished. In that regard, the season of the

Holy Ghost is a time of spiritual accountability divinely ordained to bring mankind to change course and put full focus on God. It is a new season with exacting rules divinely appointed for faithful believers only. It takes the Holy Ghost to highlight the traps and point out the way to escape the temptations that dog many in the way of faith.

It is in the season of the Holy Ghost that those proven to be worthy in the way shine to be known before men. All attempts to subvert and obstruct such no longer have effect but are easily overcome. It is in this season that the new man emerges from within the cocoon of love to soar. It is the advent of the Holy Ghost that lifts the faithful believer from a life of deigned obscurity and voluntary humility into the brilliance that turns night into noon day. All who receive the Holy Ghost are the valiant in spirit prepared as the vanguard of the new race of humanity to carry on under the banner of goodness and godliness.

The vanguard of the new race of humanity has been adopted as sons by the heavenly Father. Such are those who hear, share and obey as the Holy Ghost whispers. They belong with the living church of Christ or spiritual Israel and are the dwelling places of the Divine on earth. The heavenly Father has poured himself into all such who belong there and that is the true gift above all. He that has the spirit of the Father dwelling in him can call forth and have ready answers. He can receive whatever he wishes for through petitions and prayers. Such a one has in effect found the gold at the end of the rainbow for he has merged with light to find accord with the Divine. God's gift of himself to his sons is the ultimate for whatever the Father has his sons can also have through mercy.

It is in the season when the new is being wrought from the old that humanity is called to change ways and learn to do things God's way. Mankind has done things his way all along but the time has come for man to try doing things the heavenly way. The old becomes the new when the power of God acts through mankind in mercy. The lot of the merciful is with the heavenly Father and not with the world. Many that are still trapped in worldliness can be touched by the power of God too if they heed the plea of the voices of mercy. It is the vessel of mercy that the Father holds dear to heart and seeks to refill with the new.

Now is not the time for the seeker to look back in the manner of Lot's wife for all who do will be filled with the dregs of the sea of the world. Such will exist in a nether world and be good for neither here nor there. They will become pillars of salt that will expend their precious moments on earth on that which is sterile and fruitless. But there is still some hope for many to come away from the 'deadness' of the former into new life through Christ. Any attempt to cling to the former is to risk exclusion from the new thing that God has begun to do. All who are so excluded will remain under the veil of darkness to never wake up in the unfolding new dawn.

As humanity verges on the cusp of this new season of great spiritual unveiling, many have come into communion with God to partake of divine gifts with other saintly souls. They are the faithful who have given all so that they can come into an intimate knowledge of the Father. They constitute a spiritual brotherhood of those being perfected in the divine way to shine as points of light in a world of darkness. The greater light of God is the collective output of the light that glows from within the souls of all such and is the glorious dawn that all creation has been waiting for. Such have come to embody true light as vessels well fitted to serve divinity and humanity well.

Chapter Notes

- ✓ The faithful man is always misunderstood and under constant attack by the spiritually ignorant.
- ✓ The Holy Ghost is the means by which the Divine communicates with and reassures the faithful.
- ✓ The Holy Ghost comes to bear witness when the true believer is faced with a momentous decision.
- ✓ The Holy Ghost affirms justification before God and is given under the goodness of godliness.
- ✓ The faithful filled with divine essence has become a temple of worship and a living fountain of life.
- ✓ The imparting of the divine nature into the sons is the ultimate gift that all believers should seek after.
- ✓ The glorious dawn is the collective output of light that glows within the souls of the sons of God.
- ✓ The faithful must always be sober-minded so as to remain a worthy vessel fit for room in the Divine.

Many do compromise truth at will

And take divine grace for naught

For such life is a vain-glorious strut

A free-for-all and a feast for hogs

Chapter 9

FAITH-REST INTO RESTORATION

The life with the Holy Ghost in attendance is one lived under the mercy of the Almighty Father. It is a place for all who have forsaken the world and chosen to live by the far better heavenly way. Such are those who have come to believe the words of Truth fully and to live willingly in accordance with the divine will. As a result of that wise choice, they have grown to be strong of faith and to become fully matured in the way of Christ. To become fully matured in Christ is to be bestowed with the spiritual attributes of a son of God. Only the heavenly Father can 'christen' the believer as one worthy to stand before him as a son. It is for such who will prove to be ever faithful that he has promised to never leave or forsake. 'Christening' in light is an irreversible endowment for it bonds the faithful believer with the heavenly Father in spirit permanently. It is only when mankind has been christened in light that he will be able to give total control of his life over to God.

Christening in light affirms transformation into a spiritual image of the Divine. It is transformation that changes the inner man from the base into a purified entity over time. As the believer is changed within, the works of his hands without will come to reflect the changes that have gone on within him. As mankind's state is within, so will his estate without be. As a result, the handiwork of the believer will change over time from the ordinary to the exemplary that shines before all as he is transformed in spirit.

This comes about because the matured in spirit is tuned to hear and receive directives from above. However each one that hears in this light must lay out what he receives on a 'silver platter' so that others who are not able to obtain from the Divine can share in the feast of grace. Each one that shares in this light is a golden-hearted one who will glow from within even as his handiworks without shine before all to God's glory. His handiworks shine before humanity to enlighten and teach the heavenly ways in a world where many are spiritually blind. It takes love to urge and the touch of God to prompt the golden-hearted to carry on the works of glory on earth. On account of that love and the touch of God, the fully transformed in spirit will come into faith-rest where a host of divine helpers are available to help in his earthly endeavors.

When in faith rest, the unseen hand of God guides the faithful to accomplish earthly endeavors to Heaven's glory. It is a new and better way that makes daily living expedient. It is available to the faithful believer whose spirit is in tune with the Divine. Daily living in faith-rest does not only bring fulfillment in life but it also makes every endeavor less taxing and much easier for the faithful believer in countless ways. But such that is in faith-rest must learn to trust God fully and let Divine will hold sway over him. He must learn not to worry even in the midst of life's inevitable storms. The storms are always followed by the calm good days when the Spirit of God shows up mightily to carry out the works of glory divinely promised. Where God is duly acknowledged as sovereign, all things do always work together to bring about good outcomes at the end.

The faithful that has come into faith-rest has entered into the arena of the Holy Ghost. He must be willing to take God at his words and follow through as prompted in spirit. God has worked it all out beforehand and only seeks that human vessel worthy to be used to accomplish his divine purposes. God's purposes are always higher, grander and much farther looking than mankind can envision. Man sees only to the tip of his nose but God sees beyond the horizons on to the eternal shores. God will always use the faithful man for the better and greater than he can ever imagine or accomplish by himself. To yield to God is not only expedient but far more profitable as testimonies of all faithful believers tell. The trusting believer will always do much more with far less when the will of God dictates and governs his life.

It is indeed true that one with God can chase a thousand for the Divine multiplies and blesses the endeavors of the faithful who has learned to trust him. The believer that is acceptable for use by God is a chosen divine vehicle. The chosen vehicle of God must remain vigilant so as to spot the thorns and thistles that puncture the tires of spiritual living. He must watch out for the false confessors and not fall for their manipulative traps. They pretend to be in spiritual fellowship with the faithful but are really abusers of the divine feast of grace. They are the unfaithful and unjust flies that infect the feast for they exploit the communion of love as they would the world's offerings.

The faithful that is deemed worthy before God must therefore not be yoked with those who are still enamored with the worldly. The faithful believer that has come into faith-rest is guided under divine light and so has ceased from stumbles. He has entered the place where nothing is by chance and all that is good in creation come together to dance in the harmony of light. He has ascended into the realm where time, space, change, order, light and mist blend together in a life of regenerative splendor.

The faithful in faith-rest has entered the realm where all endeavors are carried out in the Spirit of the living God. He has entered a zone where everything works together for good for those who are called to carry out God's purposes. He has entered the 'freedom zone' where everything speaks and all things can understand each other. It is a free zone because everything speaks freely in Truth and all are woven into the fabric of eternity to hear the still small voice of life all around. It is the language understood only by the purified of heart and noble in spirit. It is the language that the divine Father uses to call his sons together even as the partridge gathers her brood.

Faith-rest is the place where God is known for all things there bear testimony to the goodness of divine love. All things pull together therein for each other in the greater and common cause of goodness. The faithful believer that has come into faith-rest is able to do the most with the least for he does nothing in his own power but does all things under the mercy of the living God. He that lives under mercy must learn to tarry and wait for God for he has embarked on a great journey. He must no longer be in a hurry to be carried about to and fro but must wait to be led in the spirit of new life that Christ has afforded.

God wants not, hurries not and therefore wastes not. The faithful is called to feed, rest and prepare for the next leg of the journey ahead for he has come into a place where man lives to accommodate God's will. It is a place where man yields way for the Spirit of God to go ahead and work things out even as the believer follows along in faith. The believer that is in faith-rest has hitched a ride on God's train of mercy that never derails for the great journey where there is much to discover and exult about.

The faithful believer who lives under God's mercy has been woven into the fabric of the ever-lasting. Such is one who will begin to speak from the wellspring of life as he lends voice to the divine spirit which dwells within him. It behooves and bodes well for mankind to listen, take note and act in kind when the merciful speak for such speak for God. It makes for better understanding to think of such as a radio receiver tuned to God's transmission frequency. All who cluster around the radio receiver will be privy to Truth that will otherwise be hidden to them. He that speaks from the wellspring of life as God's mouthpiece is one connected to the secure line used by God to send insider information to his own on earth.

The secure line of God is the Holy Ghost who comes only in the season when the divine Father is about to glorify the worthy. He comes after long years of tarrying in hope to be remade into the divine image. He comes after the faithful has been prepared and readied for victory. All the endeavors of man accomplished through the aid of the Holy Ghost turn out to be divinely glorious. There is never any doubt that it is all due to God's doing when the Holy Ghost makes a call in man's life. The heart that can hear the Holy Ghost is where the heavenly Father makes his earthly abode. The hearts where he dwells become the abode of mercy as well as the wellspring of life from where healing and restoration emanate.

Healing and restoration are the gifts bestowed on man through divine intervention. Healing comes about when man has done the best he can to find an answer to a problem but finding none looks to God for help. Healing is targeted and effected under the aegis of grace. It is an answer to a unique problem. Healing is concise, takes place in a moment of time and does not always equate to wholeness.

Restoration, on the other hand, is comprehensive and equates to wholeness. Restoration is a time function that requires time to bring about. It takes time to restore the decaying, wasting, withering and dying back to new life. It is akin to replenishing the empty or making the new out of the old. Restoration is carried out under the realm of mercy, covers everything and takes place when the believer has doubled down on faith to trust that God can indeed do the impossible through Christ.

Restoration is borne of strong faith and great vision. It comes about when the believer lives in unconditional faith and believes God for all that he has promised. Healing is a foretaste but restoration is the fulfillment of glorious living. The well informed believer with vision seeks after restoration or wholeness for such equates to new life in the fullness of light and love. For this reason, the well-informed believer is willing to sacrifice all for restoration. Restoration or wholeness is rebirth in a new life as the prize attained by the man given to obtain the kingdom of God first so that other things can be duly added on to him.

Mankind's ills and ailments are attributable to a lack of wholeness due to an underlying sinful nature. Many compromise Truth and the divine way in one form or another as they go about their daily lives. It is the compromise of Truth that invites and gives room for darkness to dwell within the heart where the Spirit of God should have been instead. The spirit of darkness is one that cripples and makes the inner man within infirm. But the faithful who loves Truth and walks on the righteous path is well prepared and fitted to overcome this spiritual malaise. The crippling spirit of darkness feeds on lies and mistruths buts beats a hasty retreat wherever God's word is embraced for it has no hiding place under the scrutiny of the light of Truth.

Restoration or wholeness is availed to the believer who faithfully embraces Truth for thereby can mankind become free from that which binds the soul to the earthy to soar upwards in spirit. Only he that has become free in spirit can ascend to the realm where righteousness is divinely imputed to the believer. Mankind must never forget that faithful obedience to Truth prepares the believer to prevail against the forces of darkness anytime and leads him from the path of the wayward on to the upward way. On a cautionary note, he that has been made righteous before God must not neglect to be merciful to others so that he can continue to live under divine mercy. He must remain merciful so as not to be choked in spirit by the roots of bitterness. He must remain merciful so that the door of mercy can remain open for him always to pass through as he goes about his daily life.

Mercy is a divine gift. Everyone that truly seeks after God will begin to recognize the attributes of godliness in the merciful. He will recognize the attributes of the Divine as laid out in the Holy Scriptures framed in the merciful for such are the righteous before God. He that has been made righteous before God is anointed or rather divinely 'magnetized' to help draw men to light. Therefore such an anointed one must be willing to carry out his role diligently for that is his life's calling. All the gifts that the righteous receive from the Father are received in mercy to be passed forward to others in grace. The golden apples of wisdom that he receives must always be served on a silver platter in love to those that seek after Truth.

He that seeks after Truth in sincerity must be willing to let God become the sovereign guide of his life. Only the true seeker willingly to trust God fully can cease from a life of sin and transgression. By the same token, he that strives to live right by God in true faithfulness will have his spiritual eye duly opened in mercy to perceive the righteous. However he that confesses falsely and seeks not sincerely will remain clouded with doubt. He will remain blind in spirit and dim of soul for he hungers not for righteousness.

As afore mentioned, the truly penitent will have the veil of blindness removed so as to begin to see clearly and know in light. He will become joined to dwell in spirit with the Divine in due time if he remains faithful to Truth. The faithful that dwells within the divine fold feeds from the trough of righteousness availed in mercy. The latter is a trough of enlightenment that has been prepared by God where the eternal truths are laid out as the fruit of the fig. All to whom the Holy Ghost is given can feed from therefrom so as to understand veiled truth communicated in figures. Such are the righteous who have been established in faith through the low hanging fruits of grace and given to eat from the uppermost boughs of mercy.

Chapter Notes

- ✓ The faithful who lives his life as informed by the Holy Ghost will accomplish the works ordained.
- ✓ The handiworks of the spiritually transformed man change from the ordinary to shine with distinction.
- ✓ A new and better way that makes life expedient comes about when the spirit is tuned to the Divine.
- ✓ The faithful that dwells within the bowel of mercy in spirit has become woven into the fabric of life.
- ✓ Healing is effected under the aegis of grace but restoration is effected under that of mercy.
- ✓ The spirit of darkness feeds on lies and mistruths but beats a hasty retreat under the light of Truth.
- ✓ The faithful that seeks after righteousness can perceive goodness in places where such exist.
- ✓ The veil of blindness is always lifted for the true seeker that ceases from transgressions to live right.
- ✓ Mercy can only be obtained from God and the receiver must ask for it in order to receive.
- ✓ The Holy Spirit is a pick-up vehicle that takes the faithful forward to rendezvous with the Divine.

Fortune's smiling face shines through

With the window of heaven fully open

So the rare gifts of goodness and mercy

Can attend to delight the chosen in love

Chapter 10

MERCY BRINGS NEW-LIFE

Only those washed in the blood of the Lamb of sacrifice are able to stand before the mercy seat of God as the justified. They are washed in the blood of the Lamb because they believed and followed after the footsteps of Christ Jesus in faithful obedience. It led them to suffer at the hands of the worldly as a result but they persevered to the end. Through belief and unwavering faith, they have come to dwell as the matured in spirit in the way of light through Christ. Along the way, they were pierced all over with the darts and arrows of a spiteful world that care little for the divine way. As a result, they are covered all over with blood flowing from the wounds of hatred that the world has inflicted on them and so belong with the flock of sacrificial lambs acceptable to God.

The lambs embody those who love God's way and live for goodness. They willingly suffer on that account so that by them others may come to reconnect with the Divine.

Although battered and bruised by the world's hatred for their love of Truth, their festering wounds do turn into the sweet smelling fragrance borne of self- sacrifice that bonds the Father and his sons together. Such is the way of Christ and that which brings mankind close to the divine heart where the justified congregate. The congregation of the justified that stand before God under mercy are those whose prayers and petitions are readily heard. The Father no longer desires sacrifices of them but rather desires that they forgive and be merciful to spiritually blind mankind.

Having given so much for love, the justified have come to live under the tender mercies of God and to have their requests readily granted. Such may not have silver or gold to give but they have divine gifts to share with those willing to embrace Truth. Their hearts have become the handle by which God touches mankind not only to forgive but to bless. He that has joined this congregation has come to live under divine providence where his needs are met and his prayers answered as due. His life is more or less on cruise control with God as the auto-pilot for he is a vessel being used to receive gifts from above in mercy and share with humanity below in grace.

The faithful that stands under mercy lives the life of the helpless that has God as his helper. He lives the life of the falsely accused that has God as his justification. It is the life of the seemingly impoverished who has access to all good things of life at his behest. He is the little one who has hitched a ride on the back of the Almighty. The batters that he has endured serve to peel away the mud cakes of the ego that encumber the flesh so that the spirit within can have ample room to grow. The flesh needs to be restrained and held in check for its impulses fight against those of the spirit. The flesh restrained makes for the spirit freed to serve God and goodness in full flourish.

Mercy drops alight sweetly as showers from Heaven. Such alight as the shower of the latter rain that refreshes the parched soul of the faithful. Mercy is reserved for those whose sacrifices are deemed to be pleasing by God. The merciful labor for God in love without murmuring and rejoice in the assurance of the abiding love and unfailing goodness that follow them through life. Mercy is tenderly dispensed from above and received freely below. Such alight in the season of fulfillment when the devourer has been cursed and kept at bay. Nothing given in mercy is wasted for the enemy cannot touch it.

Mercy originates from behind the veil of the heavenly throne of God as the portion reserved for only the noble in spirit to have. All such gifts that originate from the heavenly throne are preserved for the pure of heart for those things cannot be profaned. It is for those who love Truth and have truly chosen the way of light over the way of darkness. Mercy counts as that which the Father uses to comfort the sons of light for the troubles encountered for love of Truth and battle against the forces of darkness.

The congregation that gathers around the mercy seat of God is an elect company where there is no room found for the doubter, fence-sitter or abuser of grace. Only the certain of faith can be received into that elect company. It is the exclusive brotherhood open only to the christened in light. It is for exalted spirits fitted with the wings of the eagle. It is for those that care not for their own gain but seek the welfare of humanity. As a result, they have come into the season of their recompense and regeneration as the righteous before God. Such were misunderstood, stigmatized and suffered much hardship for love of God but have become defined as sons of God and daughters of Zion.

The righteous before God is given to hear and do God's bidding. Such is remade in the image of the Father and is a building block of the living church of Christ. He is one that has access to the precious things of life veiled to many men as well as the universal passport that grants entry into the everlasting. He is one that has gained the kingdom of God first to have other things added. The passport of life is the ultimate and much cherished gift that affirms admission into God's eternal kingdom. It is the cake of life that comes with an icing in that it affords the recipient the desires of his heart through petitions and prayer requests.

The faithful believer that has been granted the passport of eternal life is one proven worthy in the way of light through Christ. Such has carried faith's obligatory cross without counting the cost to grow in the certainty of faith that affords room in the Father's mansion. To be afforded room there is to become one in whom the divine spirit dwells or a piece of the Father's heart. It is to live the new life of the free in spirit and reborn in light for whom the universe has made everlasting accommodation.

Many who profess to walk in the light of Christ will never know the place where mankind dwells in spirit with the Father. Such partake of grace through Christ unworthily and without honor. They feast with the faithful but are unfaithful in the way on account of lust after material goods. In their haste and unbridled lust, they have sought after the reward but not the true blessing of the Father in the manner of Esau. They gain in the flesh but lack in the spirit. They seek for salvation from the wrong places for it is not obtained through the approval of men or the acquisition of the material. They are unwilling to pay the token that the way of light demands but rather seek to bargain their ways into God's kingdom.

The spiritual is not to be confused with the worldly. It may very well cost the faithful his place in the world as he seeks for a place in God's kingdom. But the faithful who obtains entry into God's kingdom first will be duly exalted to have fulfillment both in this life and the hereafter. He that has found the kingdom of God has joined the congregation of mercy. He will be entrusted with the key of knowledge that affords man greater understanding about things that pertain to the Divine and life itself. Therefore he is one given to open new doors and avail insight into life's challenges as one entrusted by the heavenly Father to lead others into better light.

Anyone drawn to embrace Truth availed through him who has the divine key will receive new sight or a fresh insight about life. He will find answers to all that bedevils him in life. The season for men to be right in their own eyes has passed. Rather the season for all to seek to be righteous before God is upon humanity for the divine help promised is at hand for the seeker after Truth. This is a time when the Divine can be heard loudly as HE tugs at the hearts of men to seek out safe haven before time runs out. Each one trusted with the divine key is a son of mercy and a voice of Truth well-prepared to guide men away from the darkness of the world into the light of God.

Wherever there is true change of heart and a committed desire to seek after God, a guiding voice will be availed to point out the right way to the seeker. Such is the nature of divine Providence. He that is committed to seek after God in true light will have an overwhelming desire for knowledge of Truth. God will always send a guide to be a bearer of light to the true seeker. There is always a 'Phillip' sent to that one in the desert that seeks to know but cannot yet find the way. Christ Jesus is the light of the world but all who have matured in him to be reborn in his spirit have become extensions of that light. Such who have followed and met up with Christ in the way are bestowed with the divine anointing that draws other men to light. It is all made possible and orchestrated by the Spirit of God both within the sharer of Truth and they that receive so that the marvelous before all is ever beheld.

The believer that truly desires to know God must embrace and love Truth. Truth affords a good measure of certainty and confidence for the believer. He that is not certain in faith will lack confidence in the ability of God to deliver as promised. The walk of faith is a partnership with the Divine that rests on the platform of Truth. Without being totally immersed in Truth, the professed believer deceives himself and has nothing before God. He that has embraced must commit the words of Truth to heart so that he can draw comfort and hope from that promised therein as he encounters opposition in the world. Commitment of the words of God to heart comes from study, meditation, praying and living by the words of Truth.

In the same wise, the believer must remain fully trusting that God will see him through his troubles when such come for it is in those times of trials that he will gain the knowledge needed to flourish and mature in the way of light. Truth that is uncompromised is the only weapon to keep the enemy at bay. He that knows the right things to do by God must do them. He that knows the wrong things not to do must avoid such. The true seeker must strive to remain righteous before God. To do otherwise is to leave an opening and give accommodation to the enemy of light and the prince of the darkness of this world. The spirit of God will become of none effect for such a professed believer who heeds not as he hears and lives not as he knows.

The follower after light often finds himself on a long and lonely path where he seems to walk alone. However he soon finds that he is not alone for a comforting voice, though unseen, always comes to affirm the traveler and whisper timely and needed encouragement to him. Nevertheless the traveler has a cross that he must carry alone even in the midst of an unseen host. The long lonely walk of faith asks the seeker to shed the trappings of the world and learn to travel lightly. It is the only way to be effective in spiritual walk. The spirit of the world expresses itself through the exaggerated self, possessions and greediness to inhibit the walk of faith. He that has made accommodation for them will not be fruitful in the way after Christ. Only unfulfilling harvest awaits all who will not yield to be pared down and commit fully to Truth but have left room in their lives for the worldly to flourish.

Mercy Brings New-Life

The believer that grows to fully mature in Christ soon becomes a righteous branch that will bear good fruits for he will be a trusted emissary of the heavenly Father to others. He will be a bearer of divine light called to hold it up so that other men may be able to see and cease from stumbling in darkness. Such is to remain a faithful witness who will not profane or gainfully use the word of Truth. Rather the bearer of light uses it as a balm to bring healing to hurting souls and as a magnet to induce other men on to the divine path by lending his voice. The bearer of light is called to speak as he hears, do as he 'knows' and go as he is sent in the Spirit of the living God. It is through such reasonable service that the power and goodness of God shows forth mightily for the benefit of humanity.

To be effective in his walk and remain faithful to his calling, the true believer must labor in voluntary humility and self-obscurity for spiritual transformation does not take place in the limelight. Wisdom counsels all attentive ears to hear that the way up is through the lowly. A man must tune out the world so that he can be tuned to hear the Divine. The traveler on the path that leads to life is like a man who willingly buries himself in the ground as a seed. The outer shell of the seed which represents the ego and such other things that mankind uses to prop up self in the world decays and is left in the ground. But by the power of redeeming glory through Christ, new life springs up from the carcass as the seedling of the new and better.

The true believer must be willing to die in his old self through Christ so that the new in the image of the Divine can come to full life within in due time. When that takes place he will be empowered as God's chosen and anointed one to model the way for those who seek but are yet to find new life. Mankind can never find new life unless he is willing to bury himself in the dust of the earth through the way of Christ. The old self is sinful and estranged from the Divine. This is the only means by which the old will be regenerated in the spirit of new life for it takes the retake of Christ to erase the mistake of Adam. Only by the retake of Christ can man get to walk in spiritual fellowship with his Creator as the righteous. He that walks with God may appear little in the world to the spiritually blind but there is great treasure in the house of such who has made himself poor to lack nothing under the mercy of God.

Chapter Notes

- ✓ The wounds inflicted on the faithful by a rejecting world can only be soothed by touch of the Divine.
- ✓ The sons may seem to be impoverished but the good in life are at their behest through prayer.
- ✓ Mercy drops are the showers of latter rain that bring regeneration to the righteous before God.
- ✓ The certain of faith endure hatred to enter into the congregation that gathers around the mercy seat.
- ✓ The righteous with the passport of life ride as exalted spirits shielded in a cocoon of love.
- ✓ The sons of light speak in love and mercy to lead men from the world's darkness into divine light.
- ✓ The faithful embrace and commit Truth to heart so that the words can spring up to life as needed.
- ✓ The bearer of greater light is called to hold it up so that men can cease from stumbling in darkness.

The challenging moments do define a man

To add up to his finest moments on earth

So a higher calling and a greater purpose

Can come to govern and dictate his steps

Chapter 11

DEATH TO AFFORD PEACE

The faithful believer that dwells under mercy is one who has spiritually grown and learned to walk on the righteous path. Such a believer is one who rests in an assurance and certain peace that is not dictated by life's circumstances but by faith. It is peace that passes all understanding and comes from the death of the old self that sometimes strove against God in the past. With the death of the old self, a new awakens that no longer strives against but yields to the divine will. When the believer spiritually matures into certain peace, he will no longer have the fear of death that weighs heavily on mankind.

To die willingly in the old self for love of God and goodness is the perfect that casts away all fears. The awakening of the new self from the death of the old is the process that completes the spiritual transformation of the wooden-hearted that is bereft of life into the golden-hearted that abounds in new life. The wooden-hearted is borne of that which is dark and foreboding. It is the spirit of death and fear. But the golden-hearted is borne of the spirit that glows in the truth of godliness. It is the spirit of life. The believer that is golden in spirit has traversed the turbulent sea of temporal life on earth and landed on the golden strand of eternity's shores. He is one bestowed with the golden touch which makes things to shine with distinction. The handiworks of the golden-hearted will always shine before heaven and earth. Such handiworks will be infused with the essence of the Divine and induce men to give due glory to God for his marvelous doings.

The golden in spirit is a model through which divine glory is displayed so that men may learn and be drawn to God. Such is one who lives for godliness and goodness. He is a son of mercy who does not boast in himself but in God. Such is given to live a life of sincere penitence, simplicity and humility. He lives in the spirit of David that seeks to glorify God above self and all things as the faithful who has learned to let the word of God dwell richly in his heart in all wisdom. He cannot help but teach, admonish and most of all sing praises to God in testimony about his unfailing goodness to mankind.

Due praise and faithful testimony about God's goodness lifts the believer into the exalted realm that affords mankind a heavenly perspective as he carries out his earthly endeavors. Praise is the common thread that binds all of God's own together. All things in creation reflect God's glory to some degree and can find common purpose through the harmony of praise to the Creator. Those that praise God sincerely will be included in the grand portraiture that reflects all who are in tune with the Divine. He that has become a part of that divine reflection has in turn been inflected into God or become merged with light so that he can know that which is veiled. He that lifts up God in praise will himself be lifted up and he that looks into the reflection of the Divine in Truth will become as the image that he sees. As the believer knows, by that will he be known and as he sees by that will he see.

Praise is the gate that lets in joy and the fulcrum upon which spiritual fulfillment rests. Praise enables the believer to achieve that point of sweet balance between the earthly and the heavenly. Mankind often hungers for the heavenly in spirit and the earthly in his flesh. As such, life becomes a struggle to achieve a good balance between the two so that man can be able to put his spiritual gifts to good use on earth and please the heavenly Father while doing so. Praise affords the believer freedom of spirit and moderation of flesh that keeps God always near. Sincere praise for God helps the mind to focus on the things above and also brings a certain reassurance that helps the faithful believer to live by the golden rule. The latter rule is embodied in the emancipating spirit of universal brotherhood where one lives for all and all for one. Praise for God makes it possible for mankind to live by the golden rule for it echoes resoundingly and warmly within the divine heart where the saintly in spirit are to be found.

The faithful believer that is at peace with the Divine has a glow that emanates from within. He glows because the sun of righteousness has risen in his soul to enable him do the marvelous in light that pleases both heaven and earth. With this sunshine within the soul availed by divine peace and Truth written in the heart, the faithful is able to produce 'honey' or such things that mankind find to be fulfilling, sustainable and enduring in life. Honey is the prize to be enjoyed after victory has been secured for God's glory and his divine purposes.

Only those who have been reborn and labor in true light can produce the works of honey for such is realized by the ability to search out veiled knowledge. Honey represents that by which God shares and bestows his glory on his sons. The storehouse of the good and perfect gifts is a honeycomb crafted by divine wisdom unlike the shortcomings of the world which are dead things contrived from the catacombs. All who are reborn in light have access to the good and perfect as the gift of honey which afford mankind pleasurable days on earth.

The works of honey are accomplished in the greater Divine light when daylight has dawned within and there are no vestiges of darkness left in the human heart. The honey season begins to unfold when mankind has learned to do all things in the light of Truth and spirit of love. It is the season when all things shine in the reflection of the Divine for all is done with purity of heart. It is the season of enlightenment and contentment where the faithful lives more to serve God's purposes but less for self. Not much is spoken in that season for all things are known and understood in the spirit. The believer will begin to hear clearly then because he has chosen wisely by faith through Christ. Therefore Wisdom has chosen to favor him with great vision and strong faith.

Only those that Wisdom has chosen in this wise can declare with certain knowledge that it is not by strength or might but in the spirit of the living God that all things should be done. They can so declare because their burdens have been lifted and weariness turned to rest through Providence. The believer that has grown to do all things in the spirit of the living God is the golden-hearted that has been welcomed into the honey season. He has entered the gilded season of life reserved only for the fully transformed in Christ. It takes many years of faithful obedience and unwavering trust in God to deliver as promised to be transformed into the golden-hearted.

Like mankind everywhere, the golden-hearted was once wooden or dead in spirit and estranged from God due to the sinful nature inherited from Adam by all. Wood is derived from a tree. The tree was once alive but being dead has turned into wood. Wood is only good for burning and so is the wooden spirit. But the wooden-hearted or the dead-in-spirit sinful man can find new life again by grace through faith. That which was only good to be burned can be turned back into the living in the light of Truth and love through Christ. The chance at redemption and resurrection into new life is God's love gift to mankind through faith. But first man must must believe and accept God's redemption plan through grace by walking in the light of Christ. Christ Jesus being the first born son of God is the iconic model through whose footsteps sinful man can find redemption and the mold by which all who are reborn are framed in divine light on to salvation.

As the believer learns and lives by the word of Truth, he will be transformed in spirit first from the wooden into the brazen stage. The brazen is the stage of sacrifice where mankind has awakened in spirit to the reality of the Divine. With this awakening comes a struggle between the old self and the newly emerging. This is where the true seeker begins to live less for self and more for God. His desire will be to do right by God. He has become a brazen altar of sacrifice. He will become keenly aware of what is pleasing to God and what is not. The ear and eye of his spirit will begin to perceive the things that are beyond the physical and his desire to experience more of the Divine will grow. But first he must overcome a deep tug of war between his flesh and the spiritual so that he can keep from transgressing and remain righteous before God. Without knowing it, he has begun a search for that sweet balance between the heavenly and earthly. He has entered into a spiritual struggle that can only be won if the seeker partakes worthily of grace and continues in good faith.

Grace is help necessary to hold up the believer and nudge him forward when he is not yet fully matured in Christ. It is more or less like holding up an infant so that he can stand firm as he takes faltering steps as he first learns to walk. Grace is divinely availed help that abounds by faith through the prayers and sacrifices of others. The latter are those who have gone before and labor in spirit to keep faith's trail of Hope open so that the way will be easier for those who follow after them. Grace manifests itself in many ways, spiritual and otherwise, in the life of the believer to help him grow in faith and commitment to God. Grace is in ever flowing abundance for the seeker in the brazen stage of spiritual transformation.

The brazen stage is only the intermediate stage of spiritual transformation. It is like the adolescent years of human development where enthusiasm and bravado abound but wisdom is scarce. However there is another stage of transformation beyond that of the brazen that many care not for much. They are too enamored with feasting on grace to pay much attention or take good notice. Beyond the brazen is the golden stage of spiritual transformation which all followers after light should desire and strive for. Therein is where mercy is availed on request and the faithful can walk on his own to stand before God as a son of righteousness. The faithful believer who tarries for transformation to the golden stage is he that will receive salvation to spend eternity with the heavenly Father.

Unfortunately most who profess to be spiritual are not able to progress beyond the brazen stage. They are not able to do so because they balk at giving everything over to God and choose rather to hold something back. They will not bless God with their best and therefore are not able to venture beyond the known horizon into the new land of promise. They settle for the gifts availed through grace but will not commit totally to become like the Giver as true faith calls. In choosing to swindle God they become abusers of grace who are like swine before him. The unworthy partaker of grace may have many possessions in this world but he will have an emptiness that will remain unfilled for he has failed to reconnect with the Father.

Chapter Notes

- ✓ Peace that passes understanding is from death of the old self that strove against God in the past.
- ✓ The son of mercy is a model by whom divine works of glory are displayed so men can be drawn to God.
- ✓ Praise is the common urge to reach out to God that brings together those that know his goodness.
- ✓ Praise enables the believer to achieve that point of balance between the earthly and heavenly.
- ✓ Only the matured in spirit can be used to infuse the earthly with essence that produces the amazing.
- ✓ The season of joy begins for the faithful when he has matured in spirit to do things in divine power.
- ✓ The struggle between the flesh and spirit can be won by grace availed by a higher spiritual power.
- ✓ In the mid-stage of spiritual transformation, much enthusiasm abounds but wisdom is scarce.
- ✓ The unworthy partaker of grace has many worldly possessions yet heaven's true gifts elude him.
- ✓ Man that has failed to reconnect with God will have an emptiness that will never be filled.

It gives man great courage to face the world

When he shares Truth from within the heart

To declare to all that there is no shame in light

But rather power therein to set the spirit free

Chapter 12

THE GOLDEN-HEARTED SHINE

Spiritual worthiness and righteousness before God is determined by the state of the believer's heart. The heart washed and purified in the fire of Truth is acceptable to the heavenly Father. It should be clearly noted by all that mankind's communion in spirit with God rests on the platform of Truth. Without truth man is but a beast and has nothing that is of value to the Divine. God is Truth and looks not for the loudest professors of faith but for heart-felt confessors. His true temple is the heart that willing suffers for love of goodness and Truth to become purified thereby. The hearts washed and purified in Truth are God's true temples and constitute his dwelling places on earth. The hearts chosen are the points of contact by which the Father's hand of affection reaches down to touch humanity on earth.

He that God chooses has become a golden-hearted one called to live in a spirit of true charity. True charity is the golden currency that is universally accepted in good faith. True charity is an act of 'burnt' sacrifice carried out selflessly for the love of humanity and goodness. True charity does not clamor for attention or the praise of men. The worthy before God are always led in spirit to empty themselves for the welfare of those who lack. The vessel that faithfully empties self for another will be divinely refilled with more and better. That is just how God does things for it is programmed into the divine economy and consciousness. All who live by true charity are the golden-hearted and noble of soul. Such are able to ascend in spirit to the most holy place of the mercy seat of the heavenly Father to ask and receive as the need arises.

The golden-hearted soul is a vessel sanctified in Truth for God's special use. Such cannot be corrupted by the evil in the world though he may be in the world for gold suffers no earthly corruption. He is one that is permanently connected in spirit with the Divine and nothing can separate that bond. Many who follow after Christ see and know in part but it is given to the golden-hearted to see and know in full. All things are made bare when mankind is bonded in spirit with the all-knowing and all-seeing Father. He that is so bonded will always be informed and endued with prescient knowledge so that he can be well prepared for life's surprising twists and turns.

Bonding with the heavenly Father comes about when the

believer has become fully matured in Christ. Spiritual maturation or transformation is a progressive process that takes place over many years. As the faithful is transformed within him from the wooden to the brazen and hopefully the golden, his handiworks will also change without to reflect the changes within him. The handiworks of the wooden-hearted or dead in spirit can be classified as works of stone. The stone work attempts to impress with sheer size. It is weighty and earthbound. It collapses under its own weight and is subject to the weathering process of heat and pressure. It is not portable so as to be shared and does not glow from within. It is showy with no discernible purpose rather than to gloat. It symbolizes work without good or justifiable purpose borne of the rebellious spirit that acts out to prove that it can be done. The stone works that dot the landscape of the past represents mankind's very early steps in embarkation on the quest for spiritual enlightenment. Stone works evoke a time in the past when mankind being barely pure in spirit is left to wonder how he can reach the stars.

As the faithful is transformed in spirit from the wooden to the next stage of the brazen, his handiworks without change as well from stone to iron works. The brazen spirit is one that has been awakened to the reality of the Divine but has not yet come into full knowledge of the heavenly ways. Such is young or an adolescent in spirit at best. By all measure the iron work is a major improvement over the stone work as much more can be done with iron in shape, size, finishing and other areas. The work of iron for all its improvements is still subject to corrosion, stress and many other outside influences. It can only resist the weather to a degree and is easily fatigued over time.

Life on earth is nothing but a continuous stress test. Iron is used by the brazen spirit to build monuments to self-accomplishments. It is the tool of the brazen spirit that will attempt anything to seek and elicit the praise of men. The iron work is the contraption that yells out man's self-congratulatory praise the loudest. It is the instrument for worshiping the creature instead of the Creator. It does not yield peace but engenders conflict within the spirit. The iron works represent mankind's second step in his quest for spiritual enlightenment. He is awake to some degree but not yet fully in his consciousness and can only leap in his attempt to reach the stars. But he cannot soar in spirit to the utmost height yet being that he is not fully awake.

But for man to be able to ascend up to the heavenly, his spirit must undergo final transformation from the brazen to the golden. As the faithful undergoes this final stage of spiritual transformation, his handiworks will change from iron to silver works. The golden in spirit has come to full knowledge and reality of the Divine Father. Silver does not corrode. It may tarnish on its surface but that can be easily wiped off. It is not used for building monuments but used rather as the service platter for mercy.

Mercy is that which can only be availed by the golden-hearted or starry in spirit. The offerings of mercy are well received above and replenished below as divine gifts that proceed from behind the veil of the mercy seat of God. The golden in spirit receives gifts from the heavenly Father in mercy to share with those that love Truth. He shares so that light and life may abound in love. He that partakes worthily of that which mercy offers will be irreversibly changed for better for he will catch a glimpse of the Divine in the enlightening reflection within its silver platter.

The silver work pleases God very much. Such is work that shines before men and is found wherever Truth is shared in love. Every silver work is composed of truth, light and love imparted into it by the golden-hearted spirit. The Father is love, the son is light and the spirit is truth. Those three shine through in the handiworks of everyone who is golden in spirit. The handiwork of the golden in spirit is enduring, pure and shines before men. Every golden-hearted one knows so much yet speaks few words. He has so much yet shows so little. He is meek but he is not afraid for to be golden-hearted is to be lion-hearted. Such is the life of the golden-hearted that he does not care to build to please self or men. Rather he carries on under the will and impulse of the heavenly Father to fashion handiworks that twinkle in light before Heaven and earth.

The Golden-Hearted Shine

The golden-hearted soul knows that he has been written into the book of life for his earthly experiences will be mirrored in the scriptures. He is fully aware that he is part of God's family for he has a new name as one called out of the world to be guided in divine light. Such is the lot of the righteous before God who walks in certainty of faith for he will pass through certain places and encounter certain situations as he completes his earthly round. It is the same journey that all the sons must complete on earth for the kingdom of God is a time worn trail ordained by the Father for the beloved and chosen. It is the golden strand where heaven and earth meet. It is the path less travelled that is parallel to the world's way. The time worn trail is ordained for those given to understand parables and veiled Truth. That which is veiled can only be understood as the faithful walk along the trail ordained for light. No one can find the trail by his own efforts. The seeker must be privy to the conversations in heavenly places before he can find it for the walk on the time worn trail is life's grand journey sustained in the light of truth by divine wisdom and love.

Chapter Notes

- ✓ The hearts chosen by God are points of contact by which his hand of affection reaches down to earth.
- ✓ True charity is borne of burnt sacrifices and is the golden currency that is universally acceptable.
- ✓ The golden-hearted is a vessel sanctified in Truth that cannot be corrupted by the world's evil.
- ✓ Full spiritual transformation is progressive and takes place in three stages over many years.
- ✓ The brazen spirit builds monuments to self-glory and will attempt anything to elicit men's praise.
- ✓ The works that shine before men are not monuments but platters to serve a divine feast.
- ✓ The sons know so much but speak little and have much but will not waste for they see in new light.
- ✓ The golden-hearted is the righteous soul before God that walks on an ordained trail of certainty.
- ✓ The golden hearted walk in increasing light that affords insightful knowledge for victorious living.
- ✓ The call of love urges the golden-hearted to share with due diligence, prudence and able stewardship.

Amazing place where heaven and earth

Touch in the embrace and kiss of love

Tis where the good gifts are exchanged

Tween enduring faith and abiding love

Chapter 13

WHERE HEAVEN MEETS EARTH

Heaven is certainly a far-away place even as earth is very near and at hand for mankind. Yet there is a place where both heaven and earth meet in love. Man can reach out there through due praise, honor and acknowledgement of the goodness of God. It has been deemed as the place of joy unspeakable and praise is the key that lifts the soul up there. The believer that always has a song in his heart and whose voice has been tuned to sing God's praise will always walk in the sunshine of divine love. Psalms and spiritual songs are not for mindless entertainment or purposeless appeals to the flesh. Rather such are expressions of the believer's experiences in his faith walk that lend testimony to the goodness and abiding love of God. The psalms and spiritual songs speak about situations that the faithful believer has been through in his spiritual walk with God. Such expressions are in fact testimonies borne of spontaneous exuberance and unsolicited candor.

Praise and thanksgiving serve as sweet candy that the faithful believer offers up in love to the heavenly Father. They flow out of self-impulse from the wellspring of the believer's heart and attest to the abiding love of an unfailingly faithful God. They serve to validate God and affirm his goodness to all that trust. They are of much relevance and comfort to all who walk after the footsteps of Christ. The places and times may vary but the experiences expressed in the psalms and spiritual songs follow the same narrative. The psalms and spiritual songs extol the efficacy of grace, the enduring nature of mercy and the infallibility of God's words of promise. They sustain both the young believer whose muscles of faith are not yet firm as well as the matured believer as he finishes out his life's work and earthly walk in testament to redeeming glory.

The psalms and hymns are like camp songs for those whose spirits have joined the congregation of the heaven bound. There are the songs piped to the children in the market place which the wise must do well to heed and dance to. The songs frame the experiences of the faithful who has taken flight in spirit to the places beyond man's flesh. There are like postcards that fill the believer with much joy and comfort for there are reminders of the places that he has been to. They fill the hearts of those who have not been with encouragement and hope that they too will someday get to such places that the songs extol. They inspire those who have not been to trust and obey so that they too may in time be lifted up in spirit to the places where the songs speak about.

The true believer who has followed after the footsteps of Christ in faithfulness to full spiritual maturity can relate to where and about what each song speaks about. The songs are like growth rings in a tree that attest to the dreary winters and cheerful summers gone by. The faithful is a tree of righteousness that has passed through certain places at certain times to encounter certain situations on the ordained trail along which all of God's faithful walk. The songs therefore paint the same portrait of a benevolent Father who dutifully watches over the sons and daughters that he has sent out to tend his garden earth. Quite often they forget to do the job and wander off for a season but soon enough they heed the call to get back and carry on with the heavenly Father's business. It is in so doing that the redeemed bring much benefit to earth and give cause for much joy in heaven.

The believer is exhorted to sing from the heart with grace because doing so is refreshingly evocative. The psalms and spiritual songs bring up memories of the faithful goodness of God in times past and serve to reassure the believer about the future. God did not fail him in the past and will not fail him in the future. At times things may not look promising or seem to be falling apart but in the long run

God never fails to fulfill his promises to the faithful man. As a matter of fact, things may not turn out as originally expected and may take longer but it is always better in the end for the faithful believer when God is involved.

It takes grace in the heart woven into songs to remind the believer about that which protects and shields him from all his troubles. It reminds him that his survival and eventual victory will not be assured by his own hands but by the provident hand availed by the Divine. It is grace that sustains and establishes the faithful in his spiritual walk until he is able to walk before God in mercy. As he sings with grace in his heart more of God's anointing is poured out so that the faithful abounds fully in spirit. Grace keeps the believer humble and penitent for he is aware that there is an unseen hand there to protect him.

Songs remind the faithful partaker that he must strive to remain a clean vessel acceptable to be used by God for diligent service. He is reminded to make himself totally and readily available for this use. Songs remind that grace is to be used for the mutual benefit of all and not be abused through selfish greed. They also encourage the faithful man to serve humanity with his best at all times and need not worry for God will always multiply those things that are sincerely sacrificed on account of love and goodness. It is for these and other reasons that the free in spirit sing in praise to the Redeemer and Care-taker above.

The psalms and spiritual songs lift the spirit of the believer up to the place where heaven and earth embrace in the kiss of love. It is a place where gifts are exchanged. The faithful believer gives to Heaven from his heart. Heaven receives from such with much approval and replenishes same with the hidden treasure. The hidden treasure of Heaven is prescient knowledge and words of wisdom whispered from above into the heart of the faithful. It is for this reason that the sweet hours of songs, study and prayer are cherished by the heart that is truly after God.

Such times are often the golden moments when the precious is received by the open and waiting heart. Each word of knowledge given and received is a key to help unlock the mystifying in life. The words bring insightful knowledge about the issues that bedevil life on earth. The enemy seeks to frustrate the believer in the small details of life so that he may lose sight of the big picture that God is working out for him. The key to defeating the enemy lies in the daily word of comforting Truth whispered in those moments when the faithful believer brings his hurting heart to offer up thanksgiving in songs and prayer to his heavenly Father in love. It is then that the divine healing balm is availed to soothe the aching heart.

The words of scripture contain pictures that are not readily discernible except by the matured in spirit. Some elements of the words of scriptures are addressed to the intellect but most are not. He that depends on his intellect to discern the words of scriptures will never get the full picture. The knowledge and wisdom that are concealed within the scriptures can only be 'figured' out by man through the understanding of the spirit. The 'truths' concealed within the words of scripture are elements of the spirit that reveal themselves only to the noble souls that have become worthy to stand before God in mercy. Such elements are pictures purposely disguised within the scriptures by the Divine to baffle the pretentious and presumptuous pithy mind of faithless man. On the other hand, such elements progressively reveal themselves to the true seeker who comes in humility and with sincere desire to know so that he can serve God to the utmost. They reveal themselves not before but after man has passed through the experiences that such truths portray.

In a way, the words of scriptures are written backwards so that it is only when viewed through the lens of experience that they come into sharp focus to be truly understood. It is only when the teachings of scripture become a lifestyle that their validity can be known to the faithful. It is only by faithful living and through hindsight borne of experience that they can become fully understood. The Truth within the scriptures cannot be surmised. Rather the scriptures should be seen as a jig-saw puzzle that can only be put together when certain keys are known. Only when the keys are known does the orderliness and harmony therein surface. The experiences which afford the believer the keys demand a lot of patience and trust to come by.

It is never easy to learn man's earthly languages even as lowly as such are. The scriptures speak a much higher and purer language that can begin to be figured out only after the mind has been washed and conditioned in Truth. It is quite a tall order to wash man's mind that is steeped in the consciousness of the world in the purifying dew of Truth. It is that difficult because the world prefers and revolves around the false white-washed as Truth. The world has become accustomed to the deceitful rubbish of the white-washed and so it becomes quite a feat to keep mankind from returning to the muddy. However God in his mysterious way does make it possible for the faithful to remain washed in Truth even in a world awash in the false that defiles many. God will cause those that he has earmarked to hear and keep Truth safely guarded at heart even in the midst of a muddy and deceitful world.

There is the world that mankind knows and lives in. Then there are the worlds of the macro universe beyond. There is also the world of the miniscule or the micro universe. In every world known and yet unknown, the same principles of orderliness and harmony hidden in the scriptures hold forth. The key that unlocks the scriptures is the same that also unlocks every other world. The over-riding Truth hidden within the scriptures is the same upon which the universe is founded. The governing order is faithfulness to Truth or that proven by time to be ever true. The same faithfulness to Truth is found in the least as well as the greatest in all things. Scale and size do not change this overriding Truth. He that is faithful to Truth is entrusted with the key of knowledge that unlocks all. He that is faithful to the true will have orderliness and harmony as governors in life. Such can re-create and transform a plot of land on earth to reflect the order and harmony in the universe. The faithful believer who is able to do that can create an earthly paradise where man and God can commune in spirit to nourish each other in abiding love.

The paradise that the faithful believer creates in his earthly plot is a reflection of the spirit that dwells within him. It is the same mind that created the universe working through him to create a little heaven on earth both within in his inner man and without in his estate. Heaven on earth is that paradise where God communes with man in spirit and speaks with him in nuggets of Truth. The faithful that has been entrusted with the key of knowledge will be connected to the source of all wisdom. All who come into the plot of paradise on earth created by such a faithful one will sense a divine presence in its midst. All who come in there will begin to hunger for God. All who come in there in good hope will receive healing and enlightenment. Such will receive the good gifts concealed therein for the true and humble seeker to find.

The faithful that has been entrusted with the key of knowledge lives his life on earth in a kingdom parallel to that of the world. He keeps faith with God on the 'strait' and narrow path even as the world rushes by on the broad and hurried way. Oftentimes he has to venture into the kingdom of the world for that is where the lost are to be found. The lost sheep of the Father's flock have to be searched for and rescued from the kingdom of the world. Each time that the faithful one ventures there, he must pass through the opposing streams of the upward bound way of God and the downward thrust of the world.

This medium of contending opposites is a sort of tornado alley. It is a very stormy place but the faithful are shielded by the golden armor of Truth and divine love. Only the strong of faith that have been chosen by God for this mission can pass back and forth through the alley without being wrecked. Only the strong of faith with spiritual vision can crisscross this alley without compromising his integrity and faith. This medium of contention is a cauldron borne of conflicting passions that would shear and tear apart the hearts that have not been sanctified in Truth.

God always take care of the faithful as he makes his forays into the kingdom of the world so that its' rising waters will not overwhelm him. Such that is shielded and sanctified by Truth becomes an intrepid vessel used by God to demonstrate his divine power and love for mankind. The heavenly Father uses the intrepid vessel on those certain days marked in his divine calendar to shame the forces of darkness into submission and show that he is ever in control of the world.

The intrepid vessel can never be sunk as 'he' sails through the stormy and battering sea of the world. Such may not be massive but it has been optimally configured to weather all storms. God often uses the things deemed little and inconsequential by man to demonstrate his power. The intrepid vessel is a representative model for all things driven by the divine wind of the Spirit of God. The divine wind will always favor the intrepid vessel so that it remains unsinkable in every circumstance and situation that it encounters. The intrepid one may encounter many storms in life but God always sees him who is on an ordained mission through. The intrepid vessel always has new testimonies to give about God's unfailing faithfulness and therefore new songs to sing in accordance.

Chapter Notes

- ✓ The believer with a song in heart and voice tuned to sing God's praise will walk in sunshine of love.
- ✓ The psalms and spiritual songs give the believer hope for they testify about God's goodness to man.
- ✓ Songs paint the portrait of a Father who loves the sons that he has sent to tend garden-earth.
- ✓ Psalms and spiritual songs serve to reassure the believer so that he may serve God with his best.
- ✓ Grace reminds that there is an unseen hand that controls all and protects humanity in love.
- ✓ The psalms and spiritual songs uplift the spirit to the place where heaven and earth embrace in love.
- ✓ Truth is wisely disguised to baffle the pretentious and presumptuous mind of faithless man.
- ✓ Scriptures speak a language understood after the mind has been washed and conditioned in Truth.
- ✓ The orderliness and harmony hidden in the scriptures hold forth and governs all in creation.

To tarry to know God's will as due

Leaves no room for fear and doubt

Helps to prepare mankind for battle

And bring him sweet victories in life

Chapter 14

BIRTH PAINS OF THE NEW

The fully matured in spirit is a golden-hearted soul that is a courier of God's precious seeds. The precious seeds of God are the seed-thoughts for the works ordained in heaven to be done on earth. Such seeds are usually entrusted to a chosen vessel and serve to further the kingdom of God on earth. The seeds are like precious pearls that cannot be entrusted to the 'swine' of the world. The precious seeds cannot be entrusted with the swindler who profanes the divine gifts for gain. They cannot be entrusted with the swindler who does not partake worthily of grace availed in the way of light through Christ.

The courier of divine seeds is guided by the spirit of God to plant in the right season and in the fruitful ground. The chosen courier is one whose heart has been lit with the flame of love that beckons mankind to the divine path. Such is that candle of God that must be held up and put on a candle stick so that other men can receive spiritual sight thereby. The heart that has been lit with the flame of love is spiritually guided on the path of righteousness to partake of the amazing in life. Such will be blessed with the good gifts of life as he lives by Truth and walk in divine light.

The path of righteousness is the trail of the new life in Christ. The chosen courier of the divine precious seeds is the fully matured in spirit within whom Christ dwells. Therefore 'He' that is being hosted within must be called to the forefront and yielded to by the courier to lead in all of life's ventures. The Christ within is called to the forefront and yielded to by request through prayer. 'He' is called forth to direct the footsteps and protect the life of the faithful at all times through the earthly journey.

Prayer is the means by which the Divine within is called forth from the hind quarters to the fore quarters of life. The effectual fervent prayer is that which cries out from the heart in humility, sincere penitence and thanksgiving. Such will always move the spirit of God to work mightily in favor of the faithful petitioner. Prayer is the medium which connects the earthly with the heavenly. The spirit cannot come in unless the heart has been opened and cannot stay unless accommodation has been suitably made. Prayer makes it possible for mankind to be tuned in spirit with the Divine. Above all things, prayer is an expression of faith in God and affirmation of the heavenly way over the worldly.

The worldly-minded soul sees no reason to pray for he trusts in his worldly goods and position in the world. He believes that those things are the walls of his strong city. But the walls easily crumble when adversity calls and the unexpected happens. The strong city of the truly faithful is not to be found in possessions and position but in the living God whose Spirit dwells within him. The heavenly Father is his strong tower both of defense to guard as well as wisdom to guide him in his earthly affairs.

The faithful that labors for God will inevitably pass through the tornado alley of life as he ventures into the world. As mentioned, it is a storm prone region that can be harrowing to the soul of the faithful. This is because the faithful is venturing from an upward bound stream where he is at home into a downward bound one where he is a stranger. The faithful laborer need not wait for the storm to show up before praying. He must first pray for the divine wind to counteract that which kindles the storm. The storm will not brew if the believer calls forth the spirit of God in faith to go before him through prayer.

It is for this reason that the faithful must keep the Divine in front and center of life above everything else. When such is the case, the divine wind is injected into the everyday affairs of life so that the storms of life are kept from brewing and their effect will be mitigated if they do. The divine wind assures safe passage for the faithful on life's harrowing sea. It is highly necessary that the faithful cultivate the use of this latent power within him for it will stay the hand of destruction that currently holds sway over much of humanity's affairs.

The world has become a raging sea that froths with unceasing and monstrous waves. Many are oblivious to the fact but it signals a separation or passing away of the old and the inception of the new. As the gulf of separation increases so do the associated upheavals. It is the very painful yet necessary birth pains of something new that has hitherto been unknown. The faithful in the way have been called and ordained to be midwives of the new creation through Christ as humanity staggers on wobbly legs into the birth of the new. A dark cloud now hovers above humanity that will break in blessing for the faithful but for the sinful it has become the foreboding season that makes men's heart to tremble with fear.

The new creation is the much anticipated golden age of Heaven on earth when the spirit of universal brotherhood will reign supreme. As pointed out already, there is a titanic spiritual struggle currently going on that is tearing the soul of humanity apart. These upheavals are forcing up monstrous repercussive waves in humanity's collective soul that leave the faithless dazed and very confused. Only the truly faithful remain untouched and unfazed by these upheavals for they abide under the protective wings of almighty God. Such will not be overwhelmed but will rather mount up with the wings of faith into the place of refuge ordained for the chosen.

Like the drunk who has denied his alcoholism for a long time, mankind is slowly but surely waking up to the fact that the earth has suffered irreparable damage. There is unanimous agreement that something cataclysmic is about to be unleashed. Belatedly mankind is coming around to the fact that it has been deceived by the enemy to choose the fool's gold of materialism above all things. Such is the fruit of the knowledge which seems good in the beginning but turns out to be evil in the end. It is the bane of humanity that mankind continues to eat from the same tree of the knowledge of good and evil that Eve and Adam could not restrain their hands from. Sadly, the forbidden has brought mankind to its knee and to the eve of demise.

All of mankind's great achievements and undertakings have led him to a dead end. Mankind is now engulfed in problems without answers. Humanity's collective soul is fractured with great schisms and degradation relentlessly eats away at all things. Mankind finds to his chagrin that he can only do so much to protect himself from the imminent catastrophe that is staring him down. He finds himself defenseless from the onslaught of disasters both natural and otherwise that he has unwittingly engendered. Each day reveals to him the increasing shortcomings and vulnerabilities of his much vaunted technology. As things shakily stand at present, the levee of mankind's collective soul is helpless to hold back the overwhelming flood borne of presumption and faithlessness that has besieged him.

The faithful who live in the light of Truth have been forewarned, prepared and readied in spirit to emerge triumphant in the coming new regime of heaven on earth. Such that walked alone with God for a long time on the path of righteousness and suffered much loss for love have been brought to life's marvelous parkway. They find themselves on the path where goodness and the tender mercies of God follow. Whereas fear, hatred and death grip the world, the faithful have come to know peace, love and the hope of eternal life. The world cries in despair but the faithful sing in contented praise to the heavenly Father. The world is boxed in but the faithful have been freed in spirit to soar into the realm of light through Christ.

The world has been on a path of self-destruction as the scriptures so accurately foretell. It has been on a 'Gadarene' rush where each man lives to gather as much as he possibly can. But the rush has led downhill into headlong destruction for many. Man has lived by the false notion that life on earth is a dash to gather material possessions and that victory belongs to him that gathers the most. His dash to gather earthly riches has led into the heart of human darkness where the golden rule is derided.

Consequently hatred and death reigns instead of brotherly love. For too long, the world's system has operated to favor the rich, the connected and the powerful. Justice exists in name only for there is really no true justice for the poor and powerless. The world's system operates in such ways that those who have more capitalize on those who have less and those who know more capitalize on those who know less. It should not be that way because as the words of scriptures explain, the favored in life are called to show love to the marginalized. This is the divine mandate that should govern earthly affairs for all humanity share the same spacecraft earth. To show compassionate love to each other is the last commandment left to his followers by Christ Jesus and that which will yet save humanity.

But today's world is a place of short-cuts, quick ways, corner-cutting and falsification where the outside appearance accounts far more than inner worth. Image has become everything as the content of a man is taken for little. The false balance of possessions, titles and connections are used to weigh men instead of morality, ethics, truth and faith. Truth has been relegated to the background in all human affairs. Whereas the light of God should have been put on a candle stick, it has been put away in the basement of humanity's soul where it does no one any good. It is the light of God that chases away dark thoughts and exposes the deeds of men. When there is light life abounds but in its absence death is empowered.

As things stand, selfishness and the motivation for personal gains have come to govern most of man's thoughts and actions. In consequence the spirit that defiles and corrupts now abounds in humanity's affairs. This manifests as the spirit of uncertainty that propels mankind all over the place in a hurried frenzy of activity from which he derives no peace or fulfillment. It manifests in other noticeable ways too to lead men to neglect to do the right things and to do the wrong instead. It also leads them to seek the company of other lost souls and to join the herd even when they know that the group is headed in the wrong direction. Such chose to die with the rest instead of having to survive alone with God if need be. Indeed, sad are the tales borne of faithlessness, lack of reverence for the Divine and the rejection of the words of Truth. The foolhardy that rejects Truth not only live with soul torn apart with guilt for rejecting the true but is denied the freedom of spirit to rise to find higher purpose.

Chapter Notes

- ✓ The precious seeds are the seed-thoughts for the work ordained in Heaven to be done on earth.
- ✓ The path of righteousness is the trail of new life reserved for hearts lit with the flame of love.
- ✓ The storms of life will be few and their effects mitigated when God is put at the forefront.
- ✓ Humanity is writhing in the birth pains of a new creation and the passing away of the old.
- ✓ The new creation is the age of heaven on earth where universal brotherhood will reign supreme.
- ✓ The bane of humanity is lust for that which is sweet and good in the beginning but bitter in the end.
- ✓ The faithful know peace, love and the hope of eternity but the faithless tread in hatred and fear.
- ✓ The light of God has power to chase away the dark thoughts of sinful man as well as expose evil deeds.
- ✓ The spirit of uncertainty propels mankind all over in frenzied activity that yields no peace or fulfillment.

The precious gifts reside in the divine showcase

As portion for faithful service in truth and love

With eternal life as affirmation and crowning glory

For the sojourner who has made the Father proud

Chapter 15

A RECLAMATION PROJECT

God's day defines those times when divine power is manifested strongly in the affairs of mankind. It is at the sunset or dusk of man's earthly endeavors that God's day commences. Divine power shows up mightily in those moments when time seems to be running out and man finds himself helpless to influence the outcome of things. It shows up readily when man finds himself seemingly out of wits and at a dead-end. It is precisely in those moments when darkness or evil seem to have the upper hand that hope re-appears as light.

Divine power is the medium for bringing hope back into the place where humanity is lost in darkness. It is by divine power that light is ushered into the darkened hearts of men so that the blind can see and the lost can find his way again. The matured believer in Christ is often led by the divine spirit to venture into the world of darkness to seek after lost souls that have been earmarked for salvation by the heavenly Father. It is therein that redeeming divine power shows forth to bring hope back to where it has vacated. But sadly mankind rarely accepts help until he teeters on the verge where all seems to be hopelessly lost.

The faithful believer through whom divine power flows in this light to change the life of others is one ordained as a rescue vehicle. He is one who has been called from a higher plane of enlightenment through the stormy divide to a place of darkness below. He is the messenger of light sent down by the divine benefactor to serve those still left in darkness. Everything always works out for the better and much good is done whenever the faithful messenger ventures out in this vein in response to the divine summons. This is the mission of rescue for which all who have been reborn in light are prepared and their lips anointed for. It is the call of Christ that will save humanity.

The faithful one who has been called to this mission of rescue from a world of darkness into light is one who lives on the heavenly side of earth. It is a calling that sets apart the obedient for a spirit-led life and affords the passport of eternity as well. He that is called in this wise must let the spirit within him take the lead in all his earthly endeavors. He can do this by request through prayer for his voice is readily heard in heavenly places. He must begin his daily walk by asking the divine spirit within to step out and take the lead in all endeavors. He must also pray for the same to guide all his thoughts, words, choices, decisions and actions. He must so pray through the day and end by praying that the same spirit stand guard through the night watch. Such is the lot of the one set apart for a spirit-led life in that the Divine wills and acts through him to make his endeavors fruitful. To depart from that is to court defeat and failures in the affairs of life.

On the contrary, the spirit that dwells within and guides the unfaithful is unclean and impure in the eyes of God. It is purposed to do work on the evil day as the thrust for divine vengeance among mankind. Such instruments of chastisement as Pharoah in the days of Moses, Nebuchadnezzer of Babylon, Judas Iscariot and such ilk all served God's divine purposes in that way. Those were the vessels of wrath created for the days of vengeance and destruction. But the matured in faith is a clean vessel of mercy created for those days when the power of God is near to bless and heal mankind through Christ.

The unclean spirit always yields to the pure in the divine scheme. It is a spiritual hierarchy that can never be violated. It is the divinely ordained order that maintains the peace of heaven and assures glory to the highest. And so it is that the spirit borne of darkness will always yield to that of light which dwells within the heart purified in Truth and lit with love. It is not possible for the unclean spirit to do otherwise for such is given to yield when confronted by the pure light of Christ. The unclean spirit is borne of darkness but the pure is evoked in light. Light and darkness can never dwell together in the same place for it has to be one or the other. Whenever and wherever true light comes to bear, darkness is always banished to a place where it can do the least harm.

The banishment of the unclean spirit is always to a place of containment where rehabilitation can be attempted. It is in the same wise as the original sentence by which the disobedient third of the angels where banished from heaven down to earth. It is the containment of the toxic and hazardous material in a desolate place where it can be decontaminated. This spiritual separation of the clean from the grips of the unclean is a reclamation project of epic proportions wrought through the spirit as light battles darkness everywhere.

The light of Christ is the pure that heaven avails humanity and has the upper hand over all else that opposes it. Having persevered to overcome the world by Truth and love, Christ is the name above all others in the spiritual realm. He has a badge of honor that affords special status and preference over all others. The unclean spirit is that of mistruths and lies. It is a devouring spirit that drags down mankind's soul into a bottomless abyss unlike the spirit of truth which lifts the soul heavenward. The message of Christ is Truth and his spirit Light that overcomes darkness.

As already noted, the unclean is the common but not the utmost spirit in the world for it is subservient to the light of Christ. The unclean is a spirit of darkness, short cuts, and quick ways that subvert the way of righteousness through the compromise and denial of Truth. It works to keep man wallowing in the mud of worldliness to make the earth his bed. For every compromised soul who has chosen the earth for a bed, the prince of the darkness of this world becomes the sovereign guide of life. Such will never ascend in spirit to the heavenly realm where the noble congregate. Such will never be counted as one among the saved worthy to stand before God in mercy.

The believer that desires escape from the entrapment of worldliness and earthiness never compromises Truth. He is one who loves to tell and hear Truth. He hates the untrue and makes no accommodation for it in his life. He knows that there is an associated cost and a prize to be paid for the love of Truth. Yet he is willing to pay that price for he has learned that God is a spirit and that the faithful must only worship him in Truth. It is Truth that marks the true believer as a faithful follower of Christ and affirms him before God. The believer can only become certain in faith when Truth becomes etched into the tablet of his heart and he lives thereby in faithful obedience.

The desire to live in Truth is the consciousness or mind-set that the faithful must have in order to be able to find new life in Christ. The embrace of Truth affords believers the means to fjord the 'Jordan' and cross into the place of promise reserved for all God's chosen. The washing of the soul in Truth must take place before purification of the spirit can be realized. The washing of the soul through Truth sets the spiritual table for the believer for it keeps the laws and promises of God foremost in mind as should be. It is kept there to remind the believer about imminent judgment and the availability of a way of escape for mankind by grace through Christ. It takes such a constant reminder to keep the believer honest, well-guarded, and faithful in his spiritual walk.

It is through such faithful obedience to Truth that the believer is able to be transformed in spirit into the new man of Christ. The transformed in spirit focuses on the exalting things in life. All that are so focused are led to choose the real over the fake and the enduring over the passing in life. The faithful who has been transformed within by obedience to Truth and by the attendant baptism of fire will come to reflect the divine image.

Such a believer that reflects the divine image is one who has matured from the child of grace to become a man of God under mercy. The child of grace is the believer that has been calibrated with the working standard of John the Baptist. The vessel so calibrated is for everyday use and often misused or abused. It is subject to violation for it pertains to lesser light that speaks to redemption into which many are called. It is in the lesser light because it is wrought by works of the flesh. It is the preparatory stage in spiritual transformation in man's bid to reconnect with the Divine. The faithful believer that lives in true faithfulness to Truth will proceed from the baptism of John which affords redemption to be calibrated with the higher reference standard of Christ Jesus which avails salvation.

Christ is the doorway into the Divine whereas John points out that door to all true seekers. By the baptism of John are many called but by the baptism of Christ, which takes place in the spirit within, are few chosen. Without the baptism of John, the believer will not be able to find the right door to meet up with the Divine and become christened in light. The christened in light or 'Christ-Man' is a higher reference standard but his faith is first proven through the preparatory standard of John. Only the one that is wrought of the higher standard of Christ is sanctified to be immune from the corruption of the world. Christening or rebirth in divine light speaks to salvation and eternal habitation with the heavenly Father. It is the gift from God that can never be violated or revoked.

The baptism of John can only take place in the spiritual wilderness. This dictates that the faithful believer will be called away into a sort of spiritual wilderness where he will be immune from a mixed-up world. It is a sort of spiritual retreat within the soul where one gets to unhitch from the unequal spiritual yokes of past associations and relationships. It is like letting go of legs and tentacles so that one can be fitted with wings. It is in this state or cocoon that the seeker will come to be truly washed by the word and have a foretaste of the pure. Only in that state will the believer grow from the immersion in Truth to be baptized in the fire of the spirit by obedience. Only the baptized in spirit will emerge with the wings that lift the believer up to meet with the Divine.

Baptism in the fire of the spirit or sanctification by Truth leads the believer into the divine presence. It is availed through tribulation and deprivation in order to affirm the believer's faith and love for God. It represents the ultimate in paring the flesh so that the spirit can abound to the utmost. The believer that does not compromise his faith but yields in long suffering patience to be remade and renamed in the new light of Christ becomes one to kept as his own or saved by God. He that is thus sanctified is protected from the corruption and evil in the world. He may be in the world but he will no longer be of it for he has become immunized in godliness on to life eternal.

Chapter Notes

- ✓ There are moments when things line up and divine power is manifested mightily to do the miraculous.
- ✓ Everything works out for the better and much good is done whenever man faithfully serves in true love.
- ✓ The impure always yield to the pure in the spiritual hierarchy for that is a universal imperative.
- ✓ The redemption of humanity is a reclamation project made possible through the divine spirit.
- ✓ The unclean spirit is prevalent in the world but it is not supreme for it is subservient to the pure.
- ✓ The faithful who desires to escape the entrapment of the world must never compromise Truth.
- ✓ The heart has to be washed in Truth before purification in the spirit of new life can be realized.
- ✓ The washing of the heart by Truth lends greater light that affords man a better vision of God.
- ✓ The matured in spirit is protected from corruption for he is sanctified in Truth and baptized in life.
- ✓ The faithful that lives on the earthly side of heaven has joined the conversation in exalted places.
- ✓ Baptism in the fire of Truth pares down the flesh minimally so that the spirit can flourish fully.

There's a ladder that leads into freedom

Joins up the earthly with the heavenly

Tis the same that lifted Jacob into Israel

From darkness below into light above

Chapter 16

A PASSPORT IS REQUIRED

The believer that is willing to be immersed in the true and pure through Christ regardless of cost has made a commitment in his heart to seek after the kingdom of God. Such a devoted soul will meet up with Christ in the way and come to the full knowledge of God in accordance with divine will. The devoted after Christ is soon bonded with the Divine in spirit for where the son is the Father may be found also. It takes baptism in the light of Truth to lead the believer to seek after the kingdom of God first so as to realize fulfillment in life thereby. To seek and find the kingdom of God is a commitment in faithfulness that takes at least seventeen years to realize. Oftentimes, it leads to the loss of one's station in the world, deprivation and rejection by many. But as always true with his promises, all that the faithful follower seemingly loses along the way through Christ is regained after the kingdom of God is realized as well as eternity as life's crown.

A Passport is Required

The tale of the spiritual trail travelled so as to afford admission into the kingdom of God is one of devotion and extra-ordinary commitment. It is quite a climb to ascend the mountain of spiritual enlightenment and should never be underestimated. The tower of faith demands a lot in spiritual resource, fortitude and goodwill in order to be completed. The spiritual traveler must be willing to forsake all in the short-term in order to meet up with Christ in the long-term. It is a super human effort that no one can accomplish without the aid of the Divine. Only the pure of heart and noble in spirit will be so aided. The divine wind helps the faithful seeker up faith's mountain so that his one can defeat the many that the enemy will throw into battle against him along the way. Only the pure of heart and noble of soul can prove worthy of the passport of life and a place in God's kingdom of light.

The believer who has been bestowed a universal passport into the kingdom of God is not bound by space and time. He can travel to distant places and realms far beyond the limits of man in spirit. Such a noble soul lives in accordance with the words of Truth written in the tablet of the heart and thereby under the guidance of the spirit embedded within those words. The life of the noble soul is anchored on the foundation of Truth. He never wanders far from the laws and commands of God so that there is a point of convergence when he becomes the words even as the words become him. It is at that point of convergence that the spirit of Truth takes over control of life so that the faithful becomes the embodiment of Truth. It is at the point of convergence that the seeker after light becomes a source of light. He has become one free in spirit that cannot help but be bound to Truth for to do otherwise is to set the spirit within to naught and be denied the victory in life that has been ordained for him.

Baptism in the spirit of Christ is baptism in the fire of Truth even on to death. It is baptism that confers certainty, universality and eternity to the spirit within man. The faithful that is baptized in the fire of Christ has become a branch of the righteous tree. The way of Christ leads the faithful through light to become a son of God in the same vein and anointing as all the others who are. The heavenly Father will not deny the request of the sons for they speak for him and carry out his will in faithful obedience.

The sons receive the passport of life as well entry into the kingdom of God with its limitless potential. Faith dictates that he that has been granted the passport of life into God's kingdom can also have anything that his heart desires from the Father. Therefore each noble son is called to stand up and bring about works on earth that bring glory to God through Christ for the divine gift of great vision with strong faith has been availed to him. He is called to desire and reach for the glorious with due thankfulness to God. He has become a man of certain faith that God uses on certain days to do the glorious in certain times and places. He is the man of faith who has cast his lot with God and not with the world. Therefore his lot has fallen on favorable places for he has become a favored recipient of the good and perfect gifts of God availed through Christ.

Sadly many erstwhile sons are lost along the way. Such are those that compromised and failed to embrace Truth wholly. By so doing, they made room for the impure spirit to come in and be accommodated in their lives. The impure is the bane of many that profess to walk in light after the footsteps of Christ Jesus. He that has become host to the impure spirit is given to substitute the praise of men for the fear of God. Such is given to keep up appearances with the worldly and play to the gallery to elicit the praise of men anytime. As a result, he soon becomes a man of uncertain bearings who is not able to find his true self in life. Rather he remains the lost soul that will never arrive at the destination divinely ordained for him in life. The fruit of the labors of the uncertain in faith is often the emptiness of unfulfilled goals and unrealized dreams. The uncertain in faith is not divinely guided in his earthly endeavors but rather does what he sees others doing. He sees no reason to live by Truth when others around him do not. Therefore, he inevitably wades into the overwhelming flood that often carries the faithless into the spiritual wasteland of hopelessness.

It is this faulted sense of identifying with the crowd that has lulled, dulled and made many to become spiritually blind. For the spiritually blind, a veil has been placed over the spiritual eye so that dimness comes to pervade the soul. The false and fake of the world now encumbers them. Such have to be replaced with the true and real of Christ if hope is to be found. This change must take place so that the light and love of the Divine can be ushered in. The believer that has met up with Christ is called to reach out in kindness so that those who have been misguided into spiritual blindness and dimness of soul can regain sight to find the way again. The faithful who can see must be the light and the guide for the blind who has lost his way. He is called to be the lamp by which his lost brother will come to see and know in light. Many who are spiritually lost in the world today will find their way again soon enough if there is a faithful one to guide them. This is the good news of redemption through the way of Christ as well as living testament to the power of sacrificial love.

Many that are lost today are victims of the impure spirit. In their ill-conceived good intentions to help things along, they seek short-cuts and take quick routes in life. As a result, they make room for the corrupting spirit of the unclean that wreaks great havoc within humanity to flourish. By making accommodation for the unclean, they compromise the core essence of goodness within mankind. They compromise the Divine spark within that defines humanity. Therefore they become the beastly of soul unable to subjugate the defiling spirit of the world rather than the pure in spirit to whom the unclean is subservient. As a result, it is no longer possible for many to discriminate between that which is acceptable in the eyes of God and that which is not as the spirit of the world now dictates most of mankind's actions. When the spirit of the world governs mankind's affairs sin abounds to have destruction and death follow suit. The faithful believer who has been freed in spirit has a mandate and divine power at his reach to help free many in the world who are still host to the unclean.

There has to be a willingness to lose one's station in the world in order for the believer to find himself and his place within the Divine. The seeker will be asked by God to make a life-changing choice between his way and the world's. It is this test of faith that many fail. It is the eye of the camel that many are not able to pass through. However the true seeker invariably chooses the assurance of the divine way over the transient and unfulfilling that the world offers. The true seekers are soon guided through the eye of the camel into the kingdom of God. Such overcome the world to break through the barrier of complexity consciousness that confines mankind to the earthly plane. They pass through into the realm of purified consciousness that governs the divine ethos as the free in spirit who have broken free of the world to live as sons of God.

He that has broken free of the world is one whose cup of bitterness has been taken away. He is one that comes in a new name to live with the peace that passes understanding and commit all his handiworks to bring glory to God. The water of Truth that washes and prepares his heart along the way duly turns into the joyful wine of marital bliss for he has become spiritually joined with the Divine through Christ. He has become host to the spirit of the Divine and in that sense dwells in the house of God. He will dwell there forever for having been joined with God through Christ his soul has become eternal. He will not dwell in the tomb of the earth as most men for he has found eternal habitation with the Father.

The entombed spirit speaks of the things that have gone before and not of the things yet to come. It can only speak of the dead and not of the living. The tomb is a dark place with severe short-comings and extreme limitations. Therefore those who dwell in the spiritual tomb seek after own gain on account of the slim pickings there. They lack great vision and are willing to sacrifice the future of their children and grandchildren for whatever they can get today. They seek safety in numbers and justify their actions by the misguided popularity of the causes they subscribe to. They live under the false sense of immunity that pronounces all actions to be acceptable if others are doing it and if it is permissible under man's laws. They have forgotten that man's only true immunity comes from the sanctity of godliness and divine justification. Such have become creatures that presume to be their own Creator and so have made themselves the arbiters of Truth and what is good for mankind. To the contrary, God is the only arbiter of Truth and knows what is best for man.

The misguided notion of living by what is popular and trendy for the season has led to the demise of all that is good in the sight of God and the assertion of might over right. In their obsessed pursuit after dainty, many have relegated the deity to the hind quarters of life and give little or no regard to divine commands. In their lust after the sweet meats of the world, they devour and hold no regard for fellow man. They see their cups of life as half-empty and are therefore hell-bent on having their fill as much and as quickly as they can. Their schemes and plots are aimed at profiting from the misfortunes of their fellow man. In taking God out of the equation, they squeeze life out of humanity and scuttle the vessels of hope. It is for this reason that mankind has come to choke under earthly possessions and muddle through life devoid of wholeness.

Chapter Notes

- ✓ To seek the kingdom of God results in the loss of much but all is restored after the seeker finds it.
- ✓ The climb up the mountain of faith is impossible without the aid of the divine Spirit.
- ✓ Baptism in the fire of Truth leads to certainty, universality and eternity of soul for the faithful.
- ✓ The fruit of uncertainty is the emptiness of unfulfilled goals and unrealized dreams.
- ✓ The faithful that meets up Christ is called to share the light so that the blind can see and find the way.
- ✓ Truth that washes the heart of the believer does turn to sweet wine of the Divine in course of time.
- ✓ The entombed spirit speaks of things from the past but the free spirit speaks of things yet to come.
- ✓ The faithless marginalize humanity and scuttle hope by taking God out of earthly endeavors.
- ✓ The lust after material possessions has caused the milk of human understanding to dry up.
- ✓ Divine bliss is to blaze new trail, find the lost, restore sight, rekindle hope and avail new life.

Soul that is in communion with God

Is an extension of the Divine on earth

And conduit for those things that flow

From Heaven's throne to earth below

Chapter 17

A NETWORK OF HOPE

The believer that is fully matured in Christ has become a son of Heaven who is connected to the universal mind of God. The son that is so connected functions more or less like a personal computer. He is connected, along with a host of other personal computers that are his sons as well, to a supercomputer God. The Holy Spirit makes available the power that energizes the system while the Holy Ghost affords the information shared within. Each son of God is given a new name which can be likened as the user identification into the network. All knowledge and needed help on how to do all things can be accessed through this network that links all the faithful that have been received into God's divine household. This is the living church of Christ and the commonwealth of the spirits of just men being perfected within the divine fold.

The sons of God have crossed the threshold from the short comings of the earthly experience into the perfecting womb of the divine experience. It is a living network akin to a beehive where all thoughts and minds blend together spiritually in a common will that serves God's divine purposes. The foremost task that each son is charged with is to seek out those that are still lost in the world who have been earmarked for salvation. It is the primary mission of the sons to find these erstwhile lost brothers and show them the way back to the heavenly homestead.

The lost ones are the square pegs trying so hard to fit into the round hole of the world. They are often oblivious of the fact that they are not of the same ilk as others who have not been earmarked for salvation. Many are the vessels of wrath but few are the vessels of mercy. It takes someone of their own ilk to remind those earmarked about the rich heritage and special privileges reserved for them within God's kingdom. It takes the son that knows how to strike up the familiar but long faded tune of old glory to lead each lost one back to the heavenly Father. The faithful who lives to help redeem the lost brother in this way will earn his heavenly stripes and divine wings.

Each son of God is charged to be an impartial judge that uses the golden rule as his standard but given to also temper justice with mercy in his dealings with mankind. He knows to be restrained as he passes judgment for all have sinned and come short of glory. He knows that there is not one good man except the heavenly Father who is perfect in every way. It is then incumbent on the sons not to rush to condemn others but to model the upward way and seek forgiveness for transgressors the best he can. Many men transgress because they do not yet know. Therefore hope should always be held out that the transgressor will come to see in better light and change his ways soon enough.

The sons of God are not readily known for who they are and what they represent. But In the course of time they come to be known for the light within them cannot be hidden. They speak with great insight into the affairs of men and future of mankind from a place beyond the commonplace. They are able to see around corners and beyond the horizon. They speak from a place of certain knowledge to bring divine light into the hidden and dark corners of men's hearts. Such words that they speak out are like arrows of Truth that pierce into hearts where sin lurks and guilt resides. The sinful heart that welcomes such Truth is led to change ways and find relief from the oppression of sin. But he that rejects same will have no hope left for redemption in this life.

The sons collectively represent man's last chance of redemption before humanity's great upheaval. Each son has been prepared to speak Truth to enlighten men's darkened hearts. The sons live as they speak as failure to do so bring them into the Father's judgment. Judgment does indeed begin within the household of God for the sword that each son carries cuts both ways. The honor of carrying the sword is reserved for the faithful few that are truly pure of heart and noble of soul. They live to please the heavenly Father and will go to any length to obey his divine will.

Each son is bestowed with divine anointing through Christ to teach Truth so that others may come to know in the light, knowledge and wisdom of God. He that has been bestowed with divine anointing is called to serve other men as God's elect on earth. His anointing is a gift from God for the benefit of humanity. It takes fortitude, wisdom and endurance to serve in this light. Therefore he that is bestowed with such anointing must seek for wisdom, vision and strong faith so as to be fruitful in his calling. Such must maintain his spiritual integrity so that no dead flies can be found in the oil of his anointing. He must remain suitably armored and make no room for the things that are displeasing in the eyes of the Father. Such mar the anointing to invite corruption and defile the spirit.

The sons constitute the Father's elite forces on earth who are informed via the Holy Ghost about where to direct their attention and mass their efforts. They are the agents being used to save the last remnant of humanity earmarked for salvation before judgment's bell tolls last. Heaven makes earthly appointments for the sons and they rally to the cause as summoned. As a result, it is their collective prayers and endeavors as guided by the Father's will that serves as the impetus to change the humanity for better. They are the gardeners of new Eden that use the power of prayer as their gardening tools to help those who love God but are choked in their hearts by the cares and worries of the world. The sons speak in little tweets of measured words but that which they speak must be received and welcomed to heart. They speak about what must be done now in a spirit of urgency that befits the times to wherever the hope of salvation yet remains. It should be noted that the sons can never be sent to those who have committed sins unto death for God is not wasteful. The latter are the truly lost who having had some experience of the Divine continue to revel in worldliness and deny the reality of God's existence.

There is a time of divine appointment ordained for all humanity. Divine appointments need to be heeded and kept. The time may be different for each but everyone on earth is given a chance to have a glimpse of the Divine. The appointed season is when God is near and can be readily experienced by those that sincerely seek to know. Such is an opportunity not to be wasted for it may never come again. It is a season when the inaudible voice of God can be easily and clearly heard. Mankind's response to that voice is a significant first step towards spiritual rehabilitation and must be obeyed when once heard in the heart. The voice that is heard always pleads with the receiver to heed the words of Truth as scripture spells out and God's commands dictate. God avails wisdom to the ready but true understanding comes with obedience to the words imparted to the hearer. He who hears and heeds will honor the hour of his visitation to his great gain. In due season, he will come to find his place within God's fold and be useful for the work of the kingdom on earth.

Those who hear and heed Heaven's inaudible yet timely call do become the building blocks of the kingdom and the vessels favored for mighty use by God. Every believer that has become a chosen vessel favored for the work of the kingdom will have the doors of Providence always open to meet his needs. The goodness and mercy of God will follow him always so that he will receive as he asks. He will knock and have the doors of opportunity opened to him as he serves the Divine will. He that has been chosen in this wise will know what to ask for and always receive the wherewithal needed to fulfill the calling.

Chapter Notes

- ✓ The faithful believer that has become a son of light is connected to the universal mind of God.
- ✓ The divine urge blends all thoughts and minds into a common will to serve God's divine purposes.
- ✓ It takes someone of the same spiritual ilk to rescue the erstwhile lost soul earmarked for redemption.
- ✓ Each son is a judge given to use the standard of the golden rule and the restraining hand of mercy.
- ✓ The honor of carrying the sword of Truth is reserved for the noble in spirit justified before God.
- ✓ The collective impetus of the wishes and prayers of the sons changes the human landscape.
- ✓ Knowledge is availed to those ready to receive but true understanding comes with obedience.
- ✓ The fisher of men is motivated by love that seeks to bring hope and restoration into man's existence.
- ✓ The sons of light find contentment on account of the goodness and mercy that follow them.

Wisdom that truly speaks to the heart

Changes not in tune or tone to please

But spirit that beguiles and misleads

Always changes pitch to suit the sale

Chapter 18

IN STEPS OF MERCY

The sons of God are given to walk under an illumination that endues them with the knowledge needed for victorious living on earth. All that each son needs to know is made known to him so that he is able to take assured and certain steps within divine will. The sons know to chase not after the transient but the enduring in life. For that reason, every son is given to take purposeful steps as one who is a model through whom God demonstrates his goodness to mankind. Many will come to believe, change their sinful ways and begin new lives through contact with the sons for it has been given to them to draw men to the heavenly way. They are able to do so not by their power or might but in the spirit of God which operates mightily through them to do the marvelous.

The sons know to be thankful for life's blessing and to remain vessels worthy of use by the heavenly Father. They also know that they have been empowered to accomplish much on earth through petitions and prayer. They can pray for forgiveness of sins and bring about healing in those that embrace Truth through Christ. Wherever the sons are well-received, much good comes about therein for goodness and mercy will attend there. Their prayer of earnest entreaty to God is given to make much available to those that embrace Truth. Each son has been elected both to offer up sacrifices and to receive blessings from the Father on behalf of humanity. Therefore each son is called to keep the doors of his heart open and live with compassion for all. It is within their hearts that the Spirit of God searches in order to ascertain what burdens are laid there so as to attend to those needs for the Father will not let his elect sons suffer needlessly.

As each son gets under the burden of another, the Divine spirit comes to buttress him. In this way, the sons appropriate God's divine power to help others. As the Spirit of the Father searches and ascertains what burdens each son, intercession is made to alleviate those problems. The heavenly Father always makes provision to meet the needs of the sons and those that embrace them. Therefore each son is called to set his heart on the things that please God so that the lovely worthy of good report may always abound through him. He is called to remain a clean vessel that is willing and ever-ready to serve God's purpose on earth. This is the reasonable service which affirms the elect sons and for which they have been prepared.

Each son of God is a vessel of mercy that must remain merciful towards humanity. He must not harbor resentments or dwell on past hurts. It must be so in order that the goodness and tender mercies of God may continue to follow him. Nothing must choke the channel of mercy for it must remain a freeway of light, love and life. The channel of mercy is the highway of the free in spirit who have overcome the world and given to ride in the high places where only few can venture. Worries, cares, grievances, resentments, grumblings, anger, envy and such emotional malware slowly but surely drag down the spirit into a stall. The stalled spirit cannot ascend and has no place on the highway of the free. He that harbors such a spirit cannot ride on the high places but must return to the low places of the earth as one who has vacated the place of honor that was appointed for him.

The measure of the spirit of each man is adversely affected by the resentments that he harbors from the past. The past is always marred and far from perfect but the future holds the promise of perfection. He that must stand in the congregation of the mighty must bid farewell to the imperfect past. He must bid farewell to the dark night of his past life so that he can wake up in the dawn of the new. Each son must forgive all in mercy for by him will the blessing of the latter rain and the tender mercies of God reach others. Wisdom declares that the blessed are the merciful for they have been given to obtain mercy. Mercy is akin to the cycle of rain. It benefits both those deemed as 'good' by men as well as the wicked. The sons live by the golden rule so as to model for both the 'good' and the wicked how things should be done on earth. It is through the enlightenment implicit in the golden rule by which they live that many come to see each other as creatures of same Creator. Many either do not know or are not sure about the heavenly way and so the few who know must demonstrate the way so others can follow.

The sons of God are called to model the way of mercy. There are no constraints or strings attached to mercy. Mercy is not constrained but flows freely with no demands attached for it is a divine gift. Mercy rejects the notion of superiority but makes ample accommodation for importunity. It seeks no rewards or accolades. It only requests to be received and shared as necessary with thanksgiving to God. It begs that hearts be opened to light and love but be closed to darkness and hatred. Mercy is indeed the last hope for beyond it is despair. Even the wicked man knows in his heart when mercy has reached him. Such is the power of the gift of mercy that it has led many wicked men to change their evil ways to seek after the Divine.

Within the core of mercy is found the goodness that covers and hides a multitude of sins as well as saves souls. The rain drop of mercy is the precursor and lifeblood of regeneration whereby the dying and broken down receive new life. The sons of mercy live by the understanding that God is in control and knows what is best for mankind in every situation. They know that God is a merciful, long-suffering, non-hasting and non-wasteful Father whose good plans for humanity are often hindered by man's impatient ways.

Many do not yet fully understand the divine way for such is much higher than mankind's. Each son must be merciful towards all for he has been called to live by a way that is higher than those of his fellows. He must ride the heavenly highway where the clouds of mercy form so that he can draw from there to be a fountain of living water for famished souls below. The exercise of mercy towards all brings the faithful believer nearer and closer to the heart of God where the fullness of divine riches is at hand. The place near to God's heart is where to receive knowledge as well as gifts to be shared in love.

The faithful believer that has come to the place close to the divine heart is under the greater divine illumination. Therefore he will have a fuller and better understanding of the Holy Scriptures. Being now in God's greater light, he is able to see the harmony in the scriptures and the veracity of its message. On a personal level, he will begin to see his life mirrored in the characters, places and events described in the scripture narratives. He will come to understand that the book of scriptures is indeed written to guide him through life. It is this understanding that enables the merciful one to settle in the place that God has reserved for him in his kingdom much as a star settles into the place ordained for it in the heavenly expanse.

The path that the faithful believer walks in life may seem to be winding and constraining but it leads the wanderer back to the heart of the Father. The heart of the Father is the fountain of life. In contrast the broad and hurried way of the world leads to the heart of darkness and death. The heart that has been led back to the Father beats in harmony with the Divine. A heart that beats like the heavenly Father's yields a mind that mimics that of the Divine. Such a heart with such a mind will be entrusted with the true riches of Heaven. Such a heart with such a mind equates to that of Christ. Such a heart with such a mind can indeed do all things with the Holy Spirit and to God's glory.

Only a few do come to know the place close to the heart of God for many are called but only a few are chosen. The few that get near are pure of heart and follow after Christ in the light of Truth. They are always willing to trust God, believe his words and pay the price for that trust for they know that they will gain the better in the long term. They are the ones despised and rejected but who walk alone regardless for they know where they are going. They are the ones crucified for love of God but who find new life through Christ. It is for them that the best has been saved for last with mercy as due inheritance.

The faithful who come close to the divine heart as well as their offspring will come to be established in righteousness through mercy. They will bring up their children with knowledge of the veiled truths upon which goodness and mercy bind themselves so that such will be like pleasurable wine to lift up their hearts in old age. All those who are established in righteousness do come into the season of restoration where the spirit of the Father is re-united with those of the children. Wisdom declares that all who come into that season will be rid and delivered from the hand of strange children whose mouths speak vanity and whose right hand is that of falsehood. Rather the sons of the righteousness will become as plants grown up in their youth to reflect the father's image and their daughters as corner-stones polished with divine attributes.

It is on this basis that the kingdom of God is founded. It is appointed for those that fear God and walk in light after Christ. It is the blessing promised in love for the man who has reverence for the Divine. All who think as the Father thinks and acts as he urges become his true children. The latter will begin to see the Father as he really is. They will find him to be an all- loving, all-knowing and all-merciful one that has their best interest at heart. This is when they will be led in spirit to become more and more like him. It is in this manner that the child becomes a man that has been remade in the likeness of the Father to enter a season of restoration and be held up as a standard for all to see.

In effect each son borne of mercy will becomes a branch of the tree of righteousness that is continuously pruned to produce even more good fruits. Each pruning season concludes with the son positioned to recreate that which he had produced on a small scale hitherto on a far grander scale. The first cycle of divine harvest is small and takes few hands to manage but the cycle that follows is always grand and requires more hands. Such is the progressive nature of the tree of righteousness in that it faithfully shows forth more branches in the passage of time. It is all by God's doing as part of that ever-lasting kingdom of peace and light of whose increase there shall be no end. It is all framed within the mosaic of eternity where all who are called must play their pre-destined part to God's glory.

Chapter Notes

- ✓ Many will change their ways and begin new lives in light through contact with the sons of God.
- ✓ Much good comes about wherever the sons of light are received for goodness and mercy follows them.
- ✓ The spirit of God searches to ascertain the burdens of the faithful in order to alleviate those needs.
- ✓ Each son of God is a vessel of mercy that must remain merciful towards all both good and bad.
- ✓ The measure of the spirit of each man is adversely affected by the resentments that he harbors.
- ✓ Mercy rejects the notion of superiority but makes accommodation for man's importunity.
- ✓ The abode of mercy is a place from which to know and receive as well as to share in thanksgiving.
- ✓ The matured under divine illumination will have a fuller and better understanding of all things.
- ✓ The path that the faithful walks is winding and constraining but it leads to the divine heart.
- ✓ Only a few come to know the realm close to the heart of God for many are called but a few chosen.

True wealth is children both natural and spiritual

God fearing fruits borne of the tree of righteousness

As the means to measure humanity's bloom or blight

To crown life's work and uphold man in his old age

Chapter 19

THE SHARER ABOUNDS

God will always provide a path of redemption for the ones whose souls he has deemed as worth saving. He will work in many and wondrous ways so that such will find the way into his kingdom. He will move the mountain in the way and hush the stormy sea as he patiently waits for them to mature in the way of light through Christ. The heart that is compassionate and merciful will always be longed after by the heavenly Father. He will not forget or forsake such whose hearts are compassionate or allow them to be lost in the world. He will work his sovereign will so that he that has a compassionate and merciful heart can find the light to lead him to the path of redemption.

The merciful heart is given to love Truth and be humble in spirit. He that will find the path of redemption must be lowly of spirit and have no hunger for the praise of men. Hunger for the praise of men leads to pride and boasting. It leads to the vaunting of self to God's displeasure. In order to please God, the believer must walk in the spirit of David as one who is sincerely repentant and truly penitent. He must embrace the message of peace and live thereby with all in love. Anyone who sincerely aspires for it will have Truth govern every area of his life. It will become part of his nature so much that he will begin to live in instinctive obedience to the teachings of Christ Jesus with little or no struggle at all. When that comes about, he will be well on his way to spiritual transformation for true light has then entered to govern his life.

Total spiritual transformation in Christ is a maturation process that takes seventeen years more or less. It takes at least that much time to come to 'master' the way of light and be led into the divine presence. It takes total commitment and devotion in the way in order to realize full maturation of spirit and rebirth in divine light. During that process the true seeker will suffer much injustice at the hands of faithless humanity. But he will overcome those and other attendant hardships to have his old nature yield to be totally replaced by the new nature of Christ. It is also during this process that he will learn to stand up for his faith. It is then that he comes to know, accept and declare boldly before all that Christ Jesus is the Master of his life. This declaration amounts to the public renunciation of the old self and taking ownership of his new self. Only when the believer has grown to do this in unfeigned humility and unabashed truth is he counted ready to battle on God's side.

The believer in whom the new man of Christ has come to full life will begin to live in a different light and with a new understanding. The ways of his old life will no longer have appeal for him but will rather begin to fade away for he has escaped his past. On the other hand, the word of God will have a new appeal and pull on his life in a way that he has never experienced before. He will grow from knowing in part to begin to know in full for he is no longer a child but a man of faith. All that he seeks to know will be shown him and all that he seeks to have will be given him as long as he no longer lives for self but for God and goodness. He may be ostracized for his faith as many will not take kindly to his new ways including family and friends. But it is by that rejection that he will come to know that he is not alone or helpless but abounding in grace. He will come to know with certainty that he is in the midst of an unseen host and to realize that ready help is at his behest for he can summon divine help as needed.

Grace is unmerited divine favor or the goodness of God that covers the believer to afford him necessary help and time to be established in faith to full spiritual maturity. The believer that is spiritually matured will grow from grace to come under the mercy of God. He is under grace when young and growing in faith but comes under mercy when he is fully matured in the way. Mercy is for the matured in faith proven worthy to stand before God in righteousness. The friends of Christ Jesus are covered under grace. If such prove to be worthy friends and embrace Truth to grow to full spiritual maturity, they will become adopted as sons of God. They will come under the mercy of the heavenly Father to become more than friends but the brethren of Jesus as well as the sons of God also.

In order to be established from grace on to mercy, the believer must devote and commit his life fully to the way of Christ. The way of Christ is about sharing and not about self. The seeker must have a sincere desire to share all that he receives through grace. He must do so in order that others may come to know about the goodness that the heavenly Father avails the faithful in the way of light after Christ. He must do so regardless of the cost for it is the sacrifice of self for the welfare of humanity that is the foundation of the way of Christ.

It is the sacrifice of self that is the true affirmation of faith and the essence of Divinity. It is a way of life that is often derided and rejected by those enamored with the worldly. They see all things in life as a business transaction and make little or no accommodation for grace. Be that as it may, wherever the sincere word is preached selflessly and not for gain, the Holy Spirit will intervene to search out and draw near those for whom Truth has been appointed. Those drawn near are the lovers of Truth foreknown from the foundation of time who are to be found in every culture, nation and peoples of the world.

Selfless sacrifice for the welfare of others is that which makes spiritual transformation possible. Only by selfless sacrifice for the benefit of others can mankind come into the experience of those things availed by the Divine. Under grace, the faithful believer knows in part. Life unfolds for him as part dream and part reality. But under mercy he will come to live the life in full that he had experienced in part under grace. Under mercy, the fully transformed in spirit can bring about anything that he desires by divine power through Christ. He will have the Holy Spirit in attendance and God's glory to affirm. This is the means by which each son is called to tell redemption's story and help reshape human affairs in accordance with the heavenly way. The world that the child of faith glimpses under grace is the world that the man of God is equipped to bring about under mercy. The door of Providence remains ever open for the man of God to receive the needs to realize his dreams under mercy. Each son must therefore be bold and never fail to ask for it has all been pre-ordained for him to receive by the Divine.

It requires nothing to come under divine mercy except a purified heart and love of goodness. The divine household is a holy place where one need not bring anything of the world into. All that the son needs to bring is his heart for worldly materials do corrupt the holy. Once he has been received into the divine household, each son can have his supplies met in mercy for he has come into Providence. His prayers will always be answered for he is held dear and near to the heart by God. He has become one who lives under the mercy of the heavenly Father whose petitions and requests will always be granted.

Each son of God has access to all that is necessary to have fulfillment in life through prayers and thanksgiving for he has been chosen by the heavenly Father as his earthly representative. It is also for this reason that he is provided with a personal assistant to provide him with real time information and knowledge about the issues of the day. This is the medium of the Holy Ghost by which he is privy to due knowledge and inside information about matters that need his attention. The Holy Ghost is the purveyor of secret knowledge and speaks from behind the veil of the throne of God into the heart of the sons. The Holy Ghost is the comforter without whom there can be no blessed assurance or fulfillment in the way in Christ.

The inner man within him matured in faith is Christ through whom victory has been ordained in all things on earth. The faithful in the way will never be able to overcome that which will confront him unless Christ within leads the battle. He will never be able to make low the mountain that stands in his way unless Christ within him takes the lead. Christ within is the one who wields the sword of victory and has all the answers for all that comes against the faithful. He is also the one that has the wherewithal to draw all the forces of light to the cause of goodness. The seekers that embrace Truth and rally to the aid of the sons in the cause of goodness will be blessed in many ways. The helpless receives help, the weary is re-energized, the depleted is refreshed and the empty is replenished when the sons are received with true love.

Each son is called to keep the flesh in check so as to give full rein to the Christ within so as to remain spiritually charged and ready for service at all times. The spirit that is fully charged is revitalized and ready to continue in the mission of Christ. The work always seems so staggering and daunting when seen with the eyes of the flesh. But the battle is not man's to fight but the heavenly Father's. God never fails to provide timely and needed help in order to make sure that the work of the kingdom gets done. The son only has to hold firm to his faith in the knowledge that all things are possible when God is involved and that the Father always finishes that which he initiates.

The work of the kingdom is often exhausting for the faithful because he commits to it totally in mind, body and spirit. Nevertheless he carries on through the ebb and flow of the spirit to produce works given to shine before all. Many who do not have experience of divine power often marvel at how God's sons are able to accomplish what they do. They are not able to fathom the means by which the faithful succeed where others fail for their wherewithal is not apparent to the spiritually blind. Their wherewithal is the power of the living God which is availed when the heart is pure and the mind is focused above.

The treasure of the sons is laid up in heavenly places where neither thieves nor robbers can touch it. The dwelling place of each son is full of great riches that only the noble in heart can perceive. It is the precious seed of Ephraim that is self-contained. It is filled with the potential for all the good and perfect gifts of life. It is the gift of the Father to recompense the son who has suffered and given up so much for love of Truth. The sons may seem to be of little stature in the eyes of the world but they are beloved and exalted in God's eye. Each is an intrepid vessel driven by the fair winds of divine fortune and fortitude.

Each son of God is a precious resource in the universe for he is a portal through which the divine impulse reaches out to humanity. His name has been written in the book of life and therefore the universe protects him through all that he encounters. He does not vaunt himself but walks humbly to hold up divine light so that all may come to know the true and pure. He is a flagship of the Divine whose course has been charted by the heavenly Father to seek out and bring home other kindred spirits marooned in the world. The lost souls who embrace Truth through the sons will in due time come to know how precious they too are in God's sight. Each son is like a gold miner provisioned by the heavenly Father to search out, dig up and help wash off the golden souls that have lain buried in the dirt of the world. The lost souls have been ravaged by the passage of time in a strange land. The sons come to find and help take them back to the treasure chest of the Father where all such belong. It is in the divine treasure chest that the redeemed find true value and are saved for eternal rest.

The sons labor so that the lost can be redeemed from the world and hopefully come into salvation to spend eternity with the heavenly Father. Each son is a light on to blind men and a beacon of hope to the hopeless. The way that he walks is not easily understood in the beginning for it is new and unorthodox. Not being the norm, the established order is often threatened by its illuminating candor. Candor can be blinding and disconcerting for the man that only knows partly and not fully. Light does not discriminate for it radiates in all directions. Any believer who comes to seek in sincerity and humility will not be denied sight. He too will come to know but he must be willing to acknowledge that which he knows to be true before men. Christ is the life and light of God given to all men as a gift. He that has experience of that light must acknowledge him openly for it is his testimony that helps to keep it ablaze so that it may shine even brighter for all. The light is found in the teaching of Christ Jesus for they contain the essence of the spirit of life and of God. He that has the words of Christ alive in him will be filled with the power of God and he that shares what he knows faithfully will come to abound in more.

Each son is a bearer of light who has been bestowed with divine anointing and empowered to do much. He that has access to the power of God must use it worthily for the benefit of all through grace. It is obtained freely with thankfulness to God and shared so that others too can benefit from it. It cannot be obtained clandestinely, bought with money or obtained through manipulation but received in grace through Truth and love. It is for the sincere of heart for it will not reject any that makes true confession and openly acknowledges the gifts received. No one who confesses Christ sincerely will be denied for true confession is the pavement of the golden way. It is not the work of man's hands that invites the Divine but the state of his heart. The heart of man is the handle by which God lifts him up but sadly the divine Father cannot touch the insincere for it is impure.

Chapter Notes

- ✓ Rebirth in light through spiritual maturation takes many years of devoted commitment to Truth.
- ✓ Selfless sacrifice so that others may come to know the divine way is God's calling on the faithful.
- ✓ The matured in spirit lives the new life fully under mercy that he had lived in part under grace.
- ✓ The faithful received into the divine household has come into the place of Providence.
- ✓ Each son lives under mercy and has access to that necessary for him to accomplish his heart's desires.
- ✓ Christ has to lead in all earthly endeavors for he is the one through whom victory has been ordained.
- ✓ The mission of Christ is daunting but the means is divine power which makes all things possible.
- ✓ The good and perfect gifts are divine's recompense for those who suffer for love of Truth.
- ✓ Every son is a precious resource in the universe for he is a portal through which the Divine spouts life.
- ✓ Each son is a gold miner that searches, digs up and washes lost souls buried in the earth for God.
- ✓ Truth can be blinding and disconcerting for the man that is spiritually blind or knows only in part.

The light of the pure and true proves ideal

For the seeds of goodness sown in love

But no other manner of seed will thrive

Under the proving rays of divine judgment

Chapter 20

THE MEAT IS THE LIFE

Anyone who has been touched by the Divine is called to share that experience with others. In doing so, he bears testimony to the reality of God's existence as well as the veracity of the gospel message. Such must play his part in the multiplication of the bread of life so that a starving multitude can partake in what God holds out in blessing for humanity. There is much to be gained in the way of Christ through sharing but on the contrary much more is forfeited by neglecting to do so. He that will not share depletes the gift and is an unworthy partaker of grace. Such is precluded from receiving more and even the little that he has will be diminished. God's gifts abound in sharing out of a pure heart for only then will the source remain inexhaustible.

The gifts and blessing of God to the believer abounds by sharing, being thankful for that received and bearing testimony to divine goodness which makes all things possible. He that will not bear testimony and give due thanks for the gift received will not be fruitful in the way for he does not acknowledge Christ. Therefore, he will not be acknowledged by the heavenly Father. It is of the utmost importance that the believer remains in good grace with the heavenly Father for he is the one that effects multiplication and brings goodness to fullness.

The believer that always acknowledges what grace avails by righteous living will be received into the mercy of the Father. Such will always find accommodation in the place close to the Father's heart. Mercy is the best that is reserved for last. Mercy comes to bear when the window of grace has closed. Mercy comes about when all has been exhausted and there is nothing more left. Mercy demands the exercise of the last muscle of faith and urges the faithful to make that last sacrifice so that he can be received into the presence of the heavenly Father. Mercy is the last preserve and the mark of validation by the heavenly Father.

God does not give up easily with his plan of salvation for lost mankind. He uses those who have been proven faithful in the way to bring about occasion for those that are lost in sin to repent. He uses all who have been divinely touched to demonstrate the truth of his person and the reality of salvation. But many refuse to take advantage of that offered in grace through the light of

Christ and thereby are denied knowledge of God. Many have good hearts but refuse to acknowledge Christ on account of shame and fear of ridicule by the world. Many others deny themselves of the offer of grace because of the fear of loss of position and stature in the world. But then they are others for whom the care and lust after materials constitute the great hurdle.

The reasons for rejecting Truth by the faithless are varied and countless but there are all attributable to the flesh. Man's flesh or his ego stands in the way and will not allow the creature to yield in submission to his Creator. Unless mankind humbles self to put aside the ego, the divine wind will blow against him for the spirit of God resists the proud. The proud can find other things in plenty but he will not find those things divinely availed. The prideful man may abound in the flesh but he will be starved in spirit. Wisdom counsels that it is more profitable for mankind to fear that which will harm the spirit. He need not fear that which will harm his flesh for in the long term the flesh profits nothing whereas the spirit is enduring. In the golden strand of the divine way, pride is a counterfeit but mercy is the real currency that serves the faithful well.

The realm of mercy is the arena of the mystifying. It is the playing field of the gods and the field of man's dreams. The realm of mercy is for the faithful who heed well the divine call and have come to live fully in the spirit of new life through Christ. The latter is a spirit of compassion that shares the burden of those that believe the word of Truth. The spirit of Christ bears the infirmity of the believer that cannot do for self and meets the helpless believer to satisfy his importunity. The realm of mercy is for those who know that it is a divine calling to help others, heal others and help save others in spite of self. The crown of mockery that such endure for doing so is that which turns into the golden crown of God's glory in due time. Indeed such that make themselves poor on account of love for God and Truth are given to have fulfillment on earth and in the after-life.

God works to bring the merciful duly into the knowledge of the precious things hidden behind the heavenly veil. The merciful that lives in faithful obedience and seeks worthily will have the door of knowledge opened to him to come into greater understanding. The heavenly Father is a God of certainty who can only use and be known by those who have put total trust in him. Divine power shows forth mightily where there is strong faith and great vision to match. It is therefore a good and desirable thing to become certain in faith for God uses such believers on certain days to do certain things in certain places. Certainty comes about when the believer has been established in grace to grow from being a friend of Christ to become his brother worthy of adoption as a son of God under mercy.

He that seeks after the light of God in Truth soon becomes absorbed into same in the fullness of time to become a man of God and a 'sun' of righteousness to enlighten the spiritually blind. On account of the fact that he seeks in love and not for selfish gain, the bearer of light in this wise is deemed worthy by the Divine to be entrusted with the precious. The precious things of Heaven constitute the body of knowledge, wisdom and enduring truths hidden away after the foundation of the world. It is in this way that God implants the eggs of his creative impulse lost in the mist of time in his sons. The hidden truths that have been lost in the mist of time make up the mysteries. The sons grow from glory to glory as they respond and utilize veiled knowledge that has been implanted within them by the Father to re-create earth in the likeness of heaven.

The hidden truths constitute the meat of the word of God. Only the fully matured in Christ can eat, digest and extract the juice of wisdom laden in them. It is knowledge held in good custody by the prudent that is not to be profaned or revealed to the unworthy. The meat of the word is like enhancement nutrition for the spirit reserved only for those souls destined for resurrection in light. The mystery and reality of resurrection can only be understood when the muscle of faith is firmed up with the meat of the word. It is the meat of the word that sustains the members of the living church of Christ. It affords the greater light that serves those who battle for God on earth so that they can overcome in life regardless of the odds against them. The meat of the word avails the wisdom and spiritual strength to press on and faithfully trust God to complete that which he has called the faithful to do.

The meat of the word is the food of eternity for it remains unchanging. Those that eat the meat of the word speak with the mind and in the spirit of Christ. They can also hear when Christ speaks through others for all the eternal souls speak the Father's language in unity of spirit borne of love. All who have come to full maturity in the way of Christ are the same kindred and speak universal Truth perceived in the spirit. The true riches of God can only be perceived and realized through the spirit. The professed believer that remains enamored with the milk of the word will remain spiritually stagnant. He will be incapable of knowing the fullness of the riches of God for it takes the meat of the word to know the higher and purer.

Christ is heard and known by the spirit of Truth. He is not known by the flesh or looks for the eyes deceive mankind more often than not. Christ steps forth from within the matured in spirit to enable him extend his vision further, his reach higher and shield him from the capricious ways of a deceitful world. Christ expresses and manifests himself to the believer that seeks after Truth in humility. The divine spirit does not look on the outside but searches within the heart for those tuned to God. It is no surprise then that the faithful within whom Christ has come to full maturity come in different colors, ages, nationalities and culture. However it is the same spirit of Christ that comes to dwell within all to register the same unmistakable imprint in the mind of all the faithful that love Truth.

All who have undergone full spiritual transformation in Christ are not known by sight but are revealed in spirit to those who have made a commitment to love God and his ways. The fully matured in Christ are ordained to show the way and provide guidance for those willing to trust God fully and accept his words of promise in accordance with the Holy Scriptures. They are called to help, lead and prepare the lost to be ready to meet the Father. The traps of fame and fortune loom large to distract many from finding the path to life. The care of the things of the world and love for the praise of men oftentimes constitute an insurmountable mountain.

The mountain stands in the way to shield the pure light of God from reaching those who need same. The mountain prevents many from receiving that which they lack and sorely need. The way of faith is littered with the countless many who gave up when victory could have been theirs to attain. Giving up when victory is at hand is a fairly common occurrence among professed believers. It results from an unwillingness to make the last sacrifice and let go of that one thing which hinders the walk. Such are those who love

God with conditions attached and will not go beyond a certain point. Unbeknown to them, the place just beyond and within reach is the realm of mercy. But there is good news to tell in that some, willing to let go of those things that hinder their way, have come to complete the journey to full spiritual transformation.

The fully transformed in Christ are the trail blazers who shine the brighter light to encourage others and afford the help needed on the way to complete the journey. The brighter light serves to expose the last vestiges of darkness so that any lingering fears and doubts harbored by true seekers can be erased. Without the help of those who have blazed the trail, the young in faith will remain in an arrested spiritual state. Such will never come to full spiritual maturity but as often as is the case will be under the delusion that they have. The complete state of spiritual transformation is to become a son of God and member of the divine household in light.

Chapter Notes

- ✓ The divine gifts abound for the faithful who shares and partakes with all out of a pure heart.
- ✓ Mercy asks the faithful to make that last sacrifice so as to be received into the divine presence.
- ✓ The heavenly Father uses the sons to frame the truth of his person and the reality of redemption.
- ✓ The divine wind of the spirit will always blow contrary when mankind is not humble.
- ✓ The realm of mercy is for the matured and faithful who has come to live fully in spirit of new life.
- ✓ The heavenly Father is a God of certainty who can be known by those who are certain of faith.
- ✓ The faithful that is certain of faith and seeks in love will come to be entrusted with the precious.
- ✓ Only the matured in Christ can eat, digest and extract the wisdom laden in the meat of truth.
- ✓ The new man within the faithful steps forth in due time to extend his vision further and reach higher.

The way of wisdom is never to discriminate

But to seek a suitable and welcoming home

It often finds the young not saddled with age

Who is noble of soul and worthy to be trusted

Chapter 21

OFFSPRING OF WISDOM

The Divine spirit is not static but remains ever dynamic. 'He' abounds and increases within the faithful believer to impact many areas of life. The fact that the faithful has come to full spiritual transformation does not mean that he has become 'perfect'. He is still growing spiritually day by day in different ways and many areas as the Divine directs him within. No one is ever perfect but God. The heavenly Father is an infinite God who has no limits. The infinite is unfathomable, unsearchable and fully unknowable. The infinite beckons ahead and the faithful can come close enough to it through the divine perfecting process. It is this desire to meet up with the Divine, which resonates strongly within faithful hearts and less so within the faithless that propels the spread of light.

The perfecting agent is the Holy Ghost that speaks to the man of God so that he may be duly informed and well prepared along life's path. The matured in spirit is endued with prescient knowledge by the Holy Ghost. He is fed with timely information from the throne of the heavenly Father about the important things to pay attention to in life. Such is availed insider information about the important in life for it seems as though a little bird whispers into his mind to brief him. He is fed the data that he needs in order to live in harmony within and with all around him. In effect, he receives constant tweets and updates from the dove of the Holy Ghost given from above. The latter speaks little but there is much said in those few words to the benefit of those tuned to hear 'Him'. It is for this reason that it is not possible for the sons or those spiritually in tune with the Divine to be deceived for they are availed pertinent information via the Holy Ghost.

Having been reborn in light, every son is free from the guilt of past sins and given to forgive all as well. As he forgives those who wrong him, both the memory and the associated guilt of his past sins fade away. He will cease to feel guilty for he has indeed become new in the light of Christ and justified before God. The new man is separate and freed from the old man of sin and guilt. He is one able to stand erect before God for he has been resurrected to sin no more. He has been given new life in order to serve God's divine will. He has become redeemed through Christ and will be kept or saved by God if he proves worthy.

The redeeming love of God availed through Christ is the

constant refrain and ever-lasting song of the faithful that has found new life. Such cannot help but bear faithful witness to what divine power avails mankind through love. All men have heard or know about God's promise of new life by grace through faith at this time. But sadly, the priceless offered in love is often ignored or dismissed by many as mere fairy tale. Such choose to join and follow the faithless throng of humanity that has no experience of the Divine. They make the popular but wrong choice of going with the crowd instead of listening to the voice of Truth within. They fear the ridicule of the world and neglect that which they know in their hearts to be true.

The truth is that God in his wisdom and mercy has infused humanity with some essence of the Divine. He has also left instructions on how mankind, if he so desires, can reconnect fully with his Creator. To God's glory many have heeded the Truth which gently tugs at the heart of every man and yielded to the divine urge. Such have left the way of the world that leads into further estrangement and turned to the way that leads back home to the Father of all. Through belief, trust, patience and commitment, they have followed the light of Christ to be guided back into the divine reality. God has become real to them as he now speaks and touches them through the heart. These are the ones who have come to know that all which the Heavenly Father speaks into the faithful heart proves to be timely and unfailingly true always.

The heavenly Father is ever faithful in fulfilling his promises to the faithful that walk on the righteous path. The pathway to God runs contrary to that of the world. Therefore to seek God in the world is to look for the living among the dead. He that runs with the 'Gedarene' herd of the in-crowd will sleep in the tomb. But he that walks towards the Divine in trust will find new life through Christ. The pathway that leads to the Father is the path less travelled. On that path the traveler may seem to walk alone but he is never really alone for he travels in the company of unseen messengers that guide, teach and encourage him. The seemingly lonely pathway leads to the mountaintop where the hidden truths lost in the mist of time crystallize and can be known. It is where night turns to day and space blends with time. It is the vortex of the creative impetus that wants not, hurries not and wastes not. Up there is the nursery of the perfect things where simplicity and orderliness attend as midwives. It is the exalted place out of which echoes the wisdom of all ages and from which the purified spirits can glimpse forwards and backwards in time as events unfold.

All who can ascend in spirit to the exalted heights have overcome the world. Eternity with the divine Father has been appointed for those who have overcome the world. Such are the ones worthy of the passport of life which grants man access to the realm of no limitations and infinite possibilities where the disciple can go further to do more than his master. But yet, it is a place where the disciple can never be above his master for the latter is in him always. The master takes the disciple along to guide him in the way so that the worthy for whom it is appointed can mature fully in light. He that has become matured must then take the old master along as the master took him along a long time ago. It is the undying reality of eternity and the saga of lives resurrected in Christ. The master dies but lives on within the worthy disciple as spiritual fathers and sons within the divine fraternal fold.

The spiritual fathers and sons do walk together in light as one as all good sons must do with their fathers. They walk together in the halls of wisdom as curators of humanity's collective goodness and redeeming grace. Their whispered voices of Truth blend together with those of the sages of the ages gone before them. Their whispered truths echo back to those seekers who follow in their footsteps. They cause all things to glow in their wake for those things that are pure do glow from within and enlighten the trail for those who follow after them. The faithful counted worthy of wisdom is able to ascertain and comprehend all Truth. It is in this way that wisdom comes to justify her children and define the men that are of good value to be sages for all ages.

The ingredient of the fulfilling, enduring and sustainable is encapsulated in the son who proves to be worthy before

Heaven. He is a faithful custodian entrusted by the Divine to be the courier of the precious things needed for regeneration. All the sons dwell in the palm of the heavenly Father as stars to be used as the foundation of the new heaven on earth. The sons will not deny or refuse whoever comes to ask of them in sincere belief and true confession. Many will be led to them in spirit for destiny always leads the earmarked on to the path of redemption. To be earmarked is to be favored through grace and it is marvelous to behold. The sons do not speak by themselves or for themselves but are rather earthly voices who relay Truth whispered into their hearts to others. They point out the way for humanity to follow and spot obstacles to avoid. In so doing, they impart due knowledge and wisdom to the ignorant so that the unwary can become aware of the dangers that lurk ahead. Those who are attentive to them have a good chance to reach the golden shores of eternity but those who do not have little.

Many in the world are spiritually sick, blind and trapped in hopelessness. The battle that dogs mankind's earthly existence, both individually and collectively, is in the spirit. The state of his spirit is manifested and can be ascertained in mankind's external surroundings. The unbelieving and faithless man fights a losing battle for he uses the wrong tools of the flesh to fight ravages visited on him in the spirit. The sons do not fight with the power and might of the flesh but in the spirit of the living God who is the final arbiter of the things that matter in life. All who heed the plea of wisdom to change ways and reconnect with the Divine will have outstanding changes take place in their lives. All who have been changed for better and proven in the fire of Truth must walk in charity and live in sacrificial love. Such must live as curators of the unchanging and enduring who live to give and receive from the spirit of the everlasting.

The lust of the flesh and earthly possessions becloud spiritual sight and debase mankind's spirit. The debased or base man is not able to perceive the spiritual for that within him is dead. The sons of God travel along on their earthly walk anonymously. They are obscured to the base man but ablaze in starry brilliance to the seeker of Truth. The true seeker need only put his faith in God and trust the word of Truth. He will be led in spirit to the source of living water for God always makes room for one more. New life will spring up in and around where there is sincere belief. But the seeker must be willing to let go of all that he has ever known for a new vista to be opened to him. Life within the divine fold is a strange new way but it holds the promise of peace, fulfillment and victory in life.

The seeker that walks after Christ must be willing to allow the Divine to take over total control and leadership of his life. He must yield as tugged in the heart and follow along as led in spirit. It is a total commitment that he must keep through all the seasons of life for he has entered into a spiritual union. It is a marriage of the willing and purified in Truth which can never be broken. The faithful believer lives continuously in Christ even as the latter lives in him. The heart of the seeker who has become bonded with Christ is much sought after and loved by the heavenly Father. Such a chosen heart will belong with God forever for he has become a son in same order as Christ Jesus.

The yoke of Christ is easy but the trail is narrow. The way of the world appears to be easy and free-willing but it leads to a dead end. Mankind should be wary for the world is a lie that masquerades as the true. Wisdom cautions all to be wary of the world's promises. Its way is to sugarcoat everything so as to mislead the blind to equate goodness with the easy and sweet. The good things in life start off difficult and challenging but end up sweet. The good things are built up on a foundation of Truth with good purpose. The good thing is taxing but pays back handsomely in the end. The good thing is borne of wisdom in the light of truth. But the ware of the world is too expensive, rewards little and wears down man's soul to nothing over time.

Chapter Notes

- ✓ The believer that is fully matured in Christ has not become perfect but has met a certain threshold.
- ✓ The sons are endued with prescient knowledge so as to be well-informed about issues that matter.
- ✓ The faithful who forgives in mercy will have the memory and guilt of his past sins surely fade away.
- ✓ The constant refrain and song of hope of the faithful should be redeeming love on to salvation.
- ✓ The sons dwell in the palm of the heavenly Father as foundation for the new heaven on earth.
- ✓ The faithless fights a losing battle when he uses the flesh to fight the ravages visited on him in spirit.
- ✓ The sons walk in anonymity on earth obscured to the faithless but ablaze in spirit to seekers.
- ✓ The heart chosen by God as a dwelling place belong in the divine fold forever as one christened in light.
- ✓ The mind of Christ can give cause to all such that brings fullness and fulfillment in life.
- ✓ The ware of the world is too expensive, rewards little and gradually wears down man's soul.

Tis better for that vessel which yields

To the wise potter that fashioned him

For only God knows what's best for man

His place on earth and the role to play

Chapter 22

REJECTED BUT WORTHY

It is not for naught that wisdom cautions all that seek in light to be ready to endure the scorn and rejection of the world. In same vein, it goes further to counsel that even the members of a man's own household will become his enemy on account of his love for God. The degree of opposition encountered and endured from family, friends and the world is often a good indication of the believer's love for God. The closer that the faithful gets to the heart of God, is the stranger that he appears to his own. But ironically this is when his love for family and friends comes to full bear for it is by his prayers that they are shielded and blessed through grace.

Following in the way of Christ requires the noble sacrifice. It requires that one should be willing to lay down his life for those that he loves. It must be done in an effaceable and selfless manner. All those for whom the faithful labors in spirit will not know in the season of planting what he is doing for them. It is only in the season of harvest, when his labors bear due fruit, that some will come to see and know. Unless it is done effacingly it will not count for much grace. Unless it comes about in this way, the faithful will never learn to walk in true charity and thereby master the divine way. True charity is that self-effacing burnt sacrifice that only a few are able to make and part of the cross that the faithful must carry along. It counts as the proofing that faith demands and that by which love is measured.

The family and friends of the faithful believer are the last ones to notice the new man of Christ that has emerged from within him. The images and impressions of the believer's old-self prove hard for them to erase for those remain stuck in their minds. The faithful should not be perplexed but must make good accommodation for such misunderstanding. He must take it all in stride in order to remain assured in peace and faithfulness. God who speaks through the thorny bush does change the thorny crown that the world puts on the believer into one of glory in due season. The father loves each faithful one even more for each hurt and injustice endured without complaint. Such are the trials and tribulation that teach about love that never gives up as well as patient hope that helps transform mankind in divine image.

Even though the light of Christ is the divine gift that counteracts the darkness in the world yet it is not easily comprehended. Those that have known the transformed believer in his past without Christ are the last to see and therefore know him in the new light of the reborn. They see him as none other but the same person gone peculiarly strange. To them he is an inconvenience to be tolerated but certainly not to be loved or embraced. They continue to view the new through the prism of the old. They lack the spy glass of faith and therefore fail to see the new man reborn through Christ. Rather he is seen as one among them who has no right to make claims to experiences different from those which they have. Sadly, they are not able to dissociate the old from the new and see the latter as a continuum of the former. They fail to recognize that the latter is a new creature distinct from the former. The old self dies in Christ so that a new and different can emerge from the carcass. Those who are in the proximity of light are the last to know. Such are prone to take light for granted and be dismissive of it.

The reborn in light are the product of profound teachings divinely inspired to transform willing mankind. They are not the products of man's scholarly systems but ordained by the heavenly Father to change humanity in a divine way. The sons are chosen not by their intellects but by their hearts. They have not gazed in its shadows and reflections but have been immersed in the true light of God. They are baptized in the wilderness of the Jordan far from the limited and presumptive teachings of orthodoxy.

They are bathed in Truth and walk in 'under-appreciated love' by their fellow men. But they know that they have been blessed with the exalted love of the heavenly Father and bear no ill will towards any man. They carry their cross nobly and walk humbly before God who has chosen them for the mission of Christ from the foundation of time. They are emissary spirits sent by the heavenly Father as pollinating bees to help those laden with promise to become fruitful in due season.

God's chosen ones do not make any claims for themselves save that Christ found, rescued, washed and purified their souls to make them worthy before God. Through that process, whereas they were previously blind they have come to see that indeed God is real and in full control. Whereas they were lame, they can now walk with true purpose on the heavenly pathway as the redeemed. They live in allegiance to the way of Christ that rescued them from a life of sin and imminent death.

Christ is really about giving in love so that the lost can be rescued from the world's darkness. In that light, the erstwhile lost now redeemed belong to the new family of the reborn through Christ who live to give all in love so that the estranged in the world can find their way home to God. All who belong to this new family embody a spiritual brotherhood forged with the blood of the Christ Jesus. It is for the noble souls who live by the by the golden rule.

The reborn are all bonded together in love for God and goodness as clones of Christ Jesus. The external looks and tongues may differ but they speak the common language of Truth in love. The hearts that love Truth understand them but the hearts that do not cannot. All who are reborn in the light of Truth share a common profile for they originate from the mold of mercy and are given to humanity as gifts from the heavenly Father. They are forged in the crucible of Truth and tempered with the blood of sacrificial love.

The sons reborn through light walk the same ancient circumambulatory trail of the ageless spirits that leads man's soul upwards from the lowliness of earthiness to the utmost reaches in Heaven. They are the cogs in the divine wheel of destiny that turns endlessly from Heaven down to earth and back up again. The divine wheel cuts a parabolic arc across the consciousness of humanity to confer divinity on those that are not afraid to walk in the light of truth and love on earth.

The order of the christened in light is governed by the everlasting spirit of Christ. He is the same yesterday, today and will so remain for all ages. He is the eternal spirit that remains in God's good grace for all ages. Most men live for one age. They are here and gone tomorrow but the sons live from age to age in spirit. They are the primordial seed held in reserve by the Father to initiate every generation of creation. They are sanctified in Truth to serve the Creator ever and yet evermore faithfully. They may be in the world but they are not of the world. Though they are rejected by their own yet all seekers of Truth know and revere them. They are the derivatives of the first born son Christ Jesus who are recreated for every age but yet remain unchanging in spirit. All who follow after the way they model will no longer be misled but will find true purpose in life.

The reborn in light must strive to keep clean from such influences in the world that corrupt and defile the spirit. He that must be of worthy service to the heavenly Father must observe the ordinances and obey the statutes as revealed to him. Ordinances have to do with the direction to follow in life. Statutes deal with the things that the faithful has to let go so that he can stand and walk triumphantly as a man of God. Statutes distinguish the man of God from the child of faith. The Christ within is greatly magnified when ordinances are observed and statutes obeyed. The observant and obedient in this wise will enter into the congregation of the mighty who are holy before God.

He that has come into the congregation of the mighty before God is a priest-king well immersed in the three dimensions of the Spirit, Son and the Father. This holy congregation is reserved for the merciful given to reign with Christ Jesus as co-heirs of the kingdom of God. The priest-king has power with God and with men. Such must make no room in life for the unclean spirit that attempts to beguile with the promise of fame and fortune. The priest-king has the Father in him. He is the dwelling place of God and his heart has been chosen for an everlasting habitation with the Divine. He that has the Father in him has everything for all his requests will be duly granted. The son that holds up the Father in the world strives to keep the impure spirit at bay so victory can always be near.

Each son upholds the heavenly Father by thinking kingly thoughts and taking princely steps. Without holding up the Father, the son cannot withstand and subjugate the impure spirit. The spirit that is subjected will serve the subjugator for the latter has become his lord. He that has the Father in him has the power to subjugate all spirits and is given the Holy Ghost as the third eye. The latter is the medium for receiving real time information needed for each moment and season. He that has the Holy Ghost will overcome that which opposes him for he has inside information and a leg up in all matters. He is well-informed and therefore well-prepared for life's battles.

The worthy believer that has come into the congregation of the mighty before God is held to a higher standard of judgment. He is judged not just as a man but as a 'god among men'. He is judged in accordance to a higher standard because he is privy to Truth that other men are precluded from. Much has been given to him and in the same wise much is expected from him. He must therefore be noble of soul and pure in spirit so that he may remain a clean vessel ready for honorable use by God. He must strive to maintain what he has been entrusted with in good stead for he has received the tool to bring forth the amazing on earth. The amazing is borne of pure thoughts as man labors not for self but to bring God due glory. Such works endure for life but those carried out for the praise of men last only for a season. The congregation of the mighty before him live to serve God's will and are therefore afforded the wherewithal to do the amazing in his name. It is for this reason that the faithful that belong therein are on a great journey where great discoveries abound and eternity crowns life.

Chapter Notes

- ✓ The faithful take princely strides and think kingly thoughts in spite of how the world perceives them.
- ✓ The faithless view the new with the prism of the old for they lack the vision imparted through faith.
- ✓ Often those that are in the proximity of light take it for granted and are often dismissive.
- ✓ The faithful belong with those that give all in love so that the lost can return to the divine fold.
- ✓ The 'brotherhood' of the noble in spirit is forged in sacrificial love and thrives by the golden rule.
- ✓ The spirit of Christ has always been and will ever be the governor of the order of the christened in light.
- ✓ The faithful is able to keep God's ordinances and statutes fully when the inner man is matured.
- ✓ The Holy Ghost avails inside information so that the faithful has a leg up in situations that matter.

Wisdom that wears the cloak of youth

Unties the leash that constrains man

Through Truth that makes the spirit free

To soar to realm of infinite possibilities

Chapter 23

CLOAK OF THE MIGHTY

The congregation of the mighty before God is called to labor together in spirit to bring restoration to the true that has been blemished over time. They are readied and prepared to refill the empty shelves of charity with that which is new, sustainable and enduring. They are equipped to upgrade the vessel of charity with that which will not break down and to replace the love that wearies in well doing with that which will not let go or give up. They come to replace that which quits when the job is not finished with that which will see the job through to the end. They come to replace that which fatigues and faints when the race is not yet completed with that which will endure till the end.

The divine wind brings the spirit of regeneration to repair the true that is broken down so that the glory of the latter may surpass that of the former. It brings the latter rain that comes when the land is dry and thirsty for new life. It brings the freed and fulfilled spirit of 'Onesimus' sent to 'Philemon' to replenish that which could not love to the end with that which can. It comes to replace that which could not bring fulfillment with that which can. The spirit of regeneration must be welcomed with due thanksgiving for it comes in mercy when hope seems to have faded.

The members of the congregation before God constitute a band of brothers in spiritual agreement who gather around the mercy seat of the heavenly Father to serve his commanding will. They have been established through grace on to full spiritual maturity through Christ. They may appear inconsequential in the eyes of the world but there are the favorite sons whom God showers with tender mercies. Above all, God has left the judgment of the world in their hands. This is to say that it is their collective spirit, which is always in agreement with the Divine, which will determine the order of the new age of man. They can be likened as the divinely ordained umpires who get to make the calls that will determine humanity's future.

The members of this congregation are fruitful trees proven to produce worthy fruits by the heavenly Father. Their life's endeavors are guided so that the kingdom of God may be firmly established on earth through them. They are led to walk in wisdom on the path of righteousness and to ride on the high places of the earth. They take the high road in all earthly matters and are travelers on the strategic pathway that God has laid out to lead mankind towards him. Nothing is impossible with God. Therefore nothing is impossible with the man whose prayers are readily answered and wishes duly granted. The mighty before God have been given the gift of the Holy Ghost and are well informed about everyday issues. As giants in the kingdom of light, they have insight into what needs to be done in every situation encountered and given to do mighty works in God's name.

The members of the congregation before God are saintly spirits who have come to know the fullness of the riches of God not for themselves but for the benefit of humanity. No one can choose that life for it does not make sense in man's way of thinking. It is a divinely ordained life and God chooses those who are called to live it. The world's system that men live by is borne of the tree of good and evil. It measures progress and defines itself by the things that show up to great applause as being good in the beginning but which eventually turn out to be less so with the passage of time. And so many of mankind's undertakings are crowned with decay and death reigns all around him. It is in that regard that the wisdom from above declares it all to be a waste of time and efforts but urges mankind rather to yield control to the Creator for the potter knows best why he made each vessel the way it is.

The beat of the world that men dance to is a marriage of

the good with the evil. Both good and evil have become intrinsically mixed up so that it is an almost impossible task to separate the two. The masters of the world know how to mask the bad to look like the good. They know that most men choose to go by sight and not by faith. Therefore the masters of the world have become like the evil shepherds who make slaughter of the sheep by promising gullible mankind much but delivering little. It is the intention of the heart that determines if the fruit is good or evil. The good deeds must be done in the spirit of pure charity for the welfare and benefit of all. Pure charity is never carried out for rewards or recognition. The desire for praise, fame or fortune must never be the motivation for such will taint charity. Pure charity is becoming increasingly rare and far between these days as man seeks new ways to win the praise of his fellows. In today's world where mankind's ego has developed a voracious appetite for praise there is an overwhelming desire to be in the lime-light and revel in self-glory whether for good or bad.

The mighty before God have been reconfigured to rule in the advent golden age of humanity. God is not about to let his cherished creation earth and favorite creature man go to complete waste. He is sorting out mankind's dross so that only the worthy will have a place in a cleansed regenerated earth. These worthy ones are those who are able to perceive with the spirit of Christ within. Having rejected the lust of fame and fortune, they have been entrusted with much by the heavenly Father so that they are fitly prepared to tend garden-earth well. They walk in the greater light of the Divine to carry out their earthly rounds protected from the evil in the world.

The mighty before God is a Colossus of faith that lives not by man's earthly ordinances but by God's heavenly laws. It is in this way that he is spiritually connected so as not to be easily beguiled and deceived by the world. They that have been bestowed with such enlightened vision are the final arbiters of all things good and evil for they go by faith not by sight. They can see the important and know the necessary in life through Divine guidance. They can perceive the futility of man's misguided efforts and manipulative undertakings. Therefore the wicked are not able to take them on the evil ride through lowly places for their spirits ride on the high places where heaven and earth meet.

The faithful believer endued with prescient knowledge, can save other believers from the wastefulness of the world's way and help them plant those seeds which will bear good fruit in time. Renewal in life comes about in that person, event or situation where the will of God dictates the steps taken. The works carried out at God's behest and dedicated to him are always established to the delight of the obedient. The mighty before God are privy to his will and as such act on due knowledge and information which they receive as spiritual memos that must be attended to. Obedience to the spiritual memo received is the work of faith that the faithful must do and encourage all seekers to do as well.

The memo of faith must always be acknowledged with due thanks for it is sent from the heavenly throne above. The divine memo is good seed that must be passed on in good faith to the ground appointed and prepared to receive it. Such seeds are appointed for the hearts that are tuned to God and hunger after righteousness. The hearts that have not turned to God but have mocked his ways will not be able to receive the divine memo for such are precluded from its knowledge. The memo contains the seed of the good things that endure and bring fulfillment to mankind. It is entrusted to the heart that is without guile and pretensions. It is entrusted to the heart that has given all to God and duly acknowledges him in all ways. The heavenly memo is received to be passed forward in good faith to those who seek after the good and perfect gifts of the Divine.

The mighty before God exemplify the best of life in Christ for they can never receive without giving back in kind. It is very useful to pray for them for the favor of God extends to those who do so. It is important to give to them for they will not use men's gifts for self but to meet the needs of the deprived. They are content in the knowledge and assurance that they can have their needs met for God readily hears them. They can lend help so many can obtain the needed in life for they commune in spirit with the Divine to offer up sacrifices as well as receive in blessing from the heavenly Father on behalf of humanity.

The mighty in faith partake of the fullness of the riches of God in a communion of spirits through Christ. The young in faith who learns to acknowledge such that are mighty in faith will have his spiritual burdens eased, share in God's blessing and be helped tremendously in his faith walk. The heart that has made room for the teachings of Christ will be shaped into a bowl that receives a good helping of the divine gifts but the heart that has denied him will not be. The mighty in faith are not hoarders but sharers of the gifts of God through Christ. They dwell in the bowel of mercy where charity makes her home and the pure of heart abide to be woven into the fabric of life to live forever in divine accord.

The mighty before God serve as guardians to re-assure those still on the way through the last leg of the wearying journey to spiritual maturation. They are like midwives that attend the birthing of the spiritual child into the man of God able to stand before the heavenly Father. They help the weary traveler to shed the encumbering not needed to complete spiritual transformation. Only the pure of heart that is not laden can finish the home stretch of the journey to join up with Christ in the Father's bosom. As each traveler arrives exhausted, the mighty in faith are the messengers who lift and accompany such in spirit as he transitions from the domain of grace into the realm of mercy. The mighty in faith embody the vehicle that picks up the weary traveler to bring him into Providence. They constitute the guardians that stand against the mocking and accusing last taunts of the enemy determined to prevent the weary traveler from coming into that which he has longed for. It is given to the mighty in faith to show up in the last harrowing moments to lift up the traveler on the triumphant shoulders of joyful brotherhood and lead him home through Christ to the heavenly Father. It is the welcoming branches of the oak trees making room for one more that has come home to join others in the forest of the righteous before God.

Chapter Notes

- ✓ The endeavors of the sons of light will determine humanity's future and place in the universal order.
- ✓ The saintly live not for self but for all so that some can catch a glimpse of the Divine through them.
- ✓ The good and bad have become mixed up in the world that it is difficult to separate them by sight.
- ✓ Heaven sorts out mankind's dross so that only the worthy will have a place in a regenerated earth.
- ✓ The matured in spirit are connected to the Divine to know the veiled and live by heavenly laws.
- ✓ The precious seed of the Divine is appointed for the ground that has been prepared to receive it.
- ✓ The sons exemplify the best of life in Christ for they always receive in mercy to give back in kind.
- ✓ The heart that has room for Truth will become a bowl shaped to receive the divine gifts.

The wise in spirit defies the limits of time

For he will be in covenant with the Divine

The young in age who is faithful and true

Will be worthy to wear wisdom's cloak

Books for Spiritual Guidance by Kalu Onwuka

Nuggets of Resurrection is an engaging discourse that explores the many gifts available to the spiritually matured in Christ, the path that seekers are called to walk as well as how to overcome challenges along the way.

Pulses of the Divine Heart is an uplifting and enriching study that attests to the abiding nature of God's love and the unfailing goodness of Providence to the faithful man whose spirit is in tune with the divine.

Etching for the Heart is a timely, fascinating and insightful study that highlights the power of sacrificial love, good hope and the enlightenment of Christ to bring wholeness in life of the believer.

No Hurry to Horeb is a thoughtful discourse about how mankind can tune his inner awareness to rise above the lowliness of today's society and realize the fullness of life divinely appointed for those who truly aspire.

Echoes of the Golden thoughtfully and deeply explores the path that leads to spiritual transformation so that mankind can begin to see from a heavenly perspective to make the earthly experience better.

Books of Original Poems by Kalu Onwuka

Anthems in the Glorious Dawn is a rich collection of ninety-three original poems to nourish the soul, uplift the spirit and help rekindle a relationship with God. The underlying message of the power of sacrificial love strikes a resonant chord.

In Enchantment of Eternity is a superb collection of ninety-four original poems that touches the heart deeply through such topics as love, the treasures of life's high road as well as the vision and victory availed through strong faith.

Tones of the Stellar is a volume of eighty eight inspirational poems that speaks to the freedom of spirit and wholeness of life availed by enlightenment through Christ. The remarkable verses offer guidance about reconnecting with God.

A Splendid Awakening is a simple yet eloquent collection of ninety-two inspirational poems that highlights how man must let go of his mistake-laden past to realize a fulfilling and enduring future full of God's blessing.

 *The Melody of Light* is a selection from the author's body of work that represents the very best of faith-based poetry. Brimming with insights and thoughtful lessons, the verses paint vivid images about the wholeness that love avails.

All titles are available as paperbacks or e-books and may be purchased through many retail outlets and on-line distribution channels including **amazon.com**. All titles may also be purchased through Granada Publishers at **www.granadapublishing.com** and excerpts of the author's work are available at **www.kaluonwuka.com**.

Kalu Onwuka is a prolific author who writes about faith-walk and the path to transformation within for better in this new age of spiritual awareness. A vanguard among the emerging breed of spiritual poets, he uses his works to highlight the path that mankind must walk in order to find a blissful balance between the earthly and the heavenly.

He is the author of *Ruminations on the Golden Strand* series which are in-depth studies based on spiritual and earthly experiences that frame modern living in a way to help mankind achieve the utmost within a relationship with the Divine. The series include *Nuggets of Resurrection, Pulses of the Divine Heart, Etching for the Faithful Heart, No Hurry to Horeb,* and *Echoes of the Golden.*

He is also the author of *Poems in Faithfulness to the Divine* series which are books of poetry and songs. These include *Anthems in the Glorious Dawn, In Enchantment of Eternity, Tones of the Stellar, A Splendid Awakening* and *The Melody of Light.* There are other works on the way including the forthcoming *Capsules of Divine Splendor.*

Onwuka is a teacher, poet, lyricist, electrical engineer and entrepreneur. He lives in California with his wife of many years with whom he has raised five children. As a follower of Christ Jesus as the Light of the world, he believes that all true spiritual paths eventually converge in Christ. He uses his writing to help many achieve spiritual transformation for a more fulfilling life.

www.ingramcontent.com/pod-product-compliance
Lightning Source LLC
Chambersburg PA
CBHW060149050426
42446CB00013B/2745